A SHORT INTRODUCTION TO PHILOSOPHY

ROBERT G. OLSON

DOVER PUBLICATIONS, INC.
MINEOLA, NEW YORK

Copyright

Bibliographical Note

This Dover edition, first published in 2003, is an unabridged republication of
the edition published by Harcourt, Brace & World, New York, in 1967.

Library of Congress Cataloging-in-Publication Data

Olson, Robert G. (Robert Goodwin), 1924–
    A short introduction to philosophy / Robert G. Olson.
      p. cm.
    Originally published: New York : Harcourt, Brace & World, 1967.
    Includes bibliographical references and index.
    ISBN 0-486-42862-1 (pbk.)
     1. Philosophy—Introductions. I. Title.

BD21.O4 2003
100—dc21

2003051651

Manufactured in the United States of America
Dover Publications, Inc., 31 East 2nd Street, Mineola, N.Y. 11501

PREFACE

THIS book was written for use in introductory courses devoted to the study of writings by the great philosophers. In contrast to conventional introductory textbooks, which are intended as balanced accounts of the history of philosophy or comprehensive and systematic analyses of philosophic issues, the sole purpose of *A Short Introduction to Philosophy* is to give the beginning student that bare minimum of perspective and critical insight without which the classic texts might prove too challenging. Depending upon the caliber of the students and the wishes of the instructor, it may be assigned either for classroom discussion in the first few weeks of the semester or as independent reading.

The approach I have followed is partly historical and partly topical. Philosophers who receive the greatest attention are Plato, Aristotle, Descartes, Berkeley, Hume, and Kant. The major issues presented are in the areas of metaphysics, theory of knowledge, ethics, and philosophy of religion. Trends in twentieth-century philosophy—pragmatism, analytical philosophy, logical positivism, and existentialism—are discussed in the concluding chapter.

I am greatly indebted to Professors Gail Belaief, Gertrude Ezorsky, and Fadlou Shehadi—each of whom read the manuscript in its first draft and made many helpful suggestions.

ROBERT G. OLSON

v

CONTENTS

Chapter One   SOME INITIAL OBSERVATIONS   3

Representative Problems in Philosophy   4
   Epistemological Problems   4
   Metaphysical Problems   5
   Ethical Problems   7
Critical and Speculative Philosophy   9
Philosophy and Science   15

Chapter Two   THE NATURE AND EXISTENCE
                OF THE EXTERNAL WORLD   19

Naive Realism   21
Representationalism   22
Metaphysical Idealism   30
Phenomenalism   33

Chapter Three   SOME REPRESENTATIVE THEORIES
                 OF KNOWLEDGE   37

Cartesian Rationalism   37
Classical Empiricism   44
Kantianism   52

Chapter Four   THE SPECULATIVE PHILOSOPHIES
OF PLATO AND ARISTOTLE   57

Plato   57
Aristotle   64

Chapter Five   PROBLEMS IN THE PHILOSOPHY
OF RELIGION   73

Some Arguments for the Existence of God   73
   The Ontological Argument   73
   The Cosmological Argument   76
   The Teleological Argument   77
   The Argument from Miracles   79
The Problem of Evil   82
Faith, Reason, and Revelation   86

Chapter Six   PROBLEMS IN ETHICS   91

Teleology and Deontology   91
The Good   99
Moral Responsibility   107

Chapter Seven   DIRECTIONS IN TWENTIETH-CENTURY
PHILOSOPHY   111

Pragmatism   111
   The Role of Intelligence   112
   Theory of Meaning   113
   Theory of Truth   114
Logical Positivism   117
Analytic Philosophy   125
Existentialism   129

A Guide to Further Reading   *135*

Index   *141*

A Short Introduction to Philosophy

𝕽𝕽𝕽

SOME

INITIAL

OBSERVATIONS

THE word *philosophy* comes from two Greek words: *philia* (love) and *sophia* (wisdom). Originally it meant almost any inquiry that required intellectual effort. In the Middle Ages the meaning of the term somewhat narrowed, but philosophy was still called "the queen of the sciences." Even in the seventeenth and eighteenth centuries the word was employed broadly. Newton's major work, for instance, was entitled *Mathematical Principles of Natural Philosophy*. Today, however, few philosophers would style themselves "lovers of wisdom," and most searchers after knowledge lay no claim at all to the title of philosopher.

Largely because of its rich heritage, any brief definition of philosophy would be either too controversial or too vague to serve a useful purpose. The nature of philosophy has itself become a philosophical problem—one to which sharply conflicting answers have been given. Bertrand Russell has held that philosophy is essentially the forerunner of science. Its subject matter consists of vaguely formulated problems with which science in its present stage of development cannot cope. As soon, however, as philosophers succeed in clearly stating a problem, thereby opening the way to its satisfactory resolution, the problem passes from the domain of philosophy to the domain of science. Many logical positivists regard the philosopher's principal job to be that of examining critically the methods employed in the established sciences in order to discover their rationale and ultimately to refine them. According to contemporary existentialists, the task of philosophy is to define what they call "the human condition": the pervasive traits of human existence and the basic ways in which men relate to one another and to the world. According to adherents of analytic philosophy, the movement which today is dominant in England and America, philosophy ought to be restricted to the analysis of language. Many Marxists argue that philosophy consists largely of ideologies designed to justify and maintain positions of power and privilege for some ruling class. For John Dewey, a leading pragmatist, the essential role of the philosopher is to analyze and appraise his society with a view to improving it.

Still other views of philosophy could be enumerated, but it should already be clear that any adequate introduction to philosophy will be less tidy and systematic than introductions to more clearly defined intellectual disciplines. In this chapter we shall (1) set down some typical problems in three of the major branches of philosophy, (2) discuss briefly the distinctive approaches philosophers have adopted in dealing with their subject matter, and (3) point out some of the important ways in which philosophy differs from science. Though this chapter cannot be regarded as a definition of philosophy, it will provide a loose frame of reference for the problems discussed in later chapters and will also acquaint the reader with a number of helpful technical terms.

REPRESENTATIVE PROBLEMS IN PHILOSOPHY

Epistemological Problems. In the modern period of philosophy, commonly said to have begun with the seventeenth-century French philosopher René Descartes, the branch of philosophy that has been most to the fore is *theory of knowledge* or *epistemology*. Typically, the epistemologist asks three major questions: (1) "What are the principal grounds of knowledge?" (2) "How certain can we properly be of what we think we know?" and (3) "Are there limits beyond which we cannot reasonably hope to extend knowledge?"

Debate on the first of these three questions turns chiefly upon the relative roles of unaided reason and of perception through the physical senses. Depending upon which of these two avenues of knowledge is most heavily stressed, a theory of knowledge is classified as *rationalist* or *empiricist*. If a philosopher believes that the unaided use of human reason is the principal ground of knowledge, he is called a *rationalist*. If he emphasizes the role of the physical senses he is an *empiricist*. Descartes, who seemed never to tire of warning against reliance upon the physical senses, was a rationalist. David Hume, an eighteenth-century British philosopher who repeatedly affirmed that no matters of fact could be known to be true without an appeal to the senses, was an empiricist.

The second and third questions, relating to the degree of certainty and the extent of human knowledge, have both received many different answers. In general, however, rationalists tend to the view that men may acquire entirely certain knowledge of almost anything they care to know—be it the ultimate nature of the universe, the existence of God, the laws of nature, or moral law. Most of them have been deeply impressed by mathematics and have argued first that the mental faculties used to discover the truths of mathematics are adequate to discover truth in other areas of human inquiry, and second that genuine knowledge in any field is as certain as mathematical truths. Socrates and Plato—the first of the great philosophers, who lived in Athens in the fifth century B.C.—refused to use the word *knowledge* for any beliefs which fell short of absolute certainty; those that did they called *opinions*. Descartes made the same distinction.

Empiricists, on the contrary, have argued that complete certainty is unattainable outside mathematics and formal logic. Many of them have denied the possibility of acquiring any reliable knowledge at all about ultimate reality or about morals. Practically all have insisted that knowledge of natural events and the laws governing them is merely probable. In some cases the probability is so high that for practical purposes doubts may be safely set aside, but future experience may always prove us wrong.

Metaphysical Problems. A second major branch of philosophy is *metaphysics*. The term itself has a curious history. Aristotle,

a Greek philosopher who studied under Plato and ranks with
him in importance, is known to us today through a series of
works, apparently taken from lecture notes, published some time
after his death. The titles of the volumes in this series were chosen
by the editors, who had little trouble finding appropriate titles
for most of them—*On the Soul, Physics, The History of Animals,*
for example—but the volume that followed *Physics* presented a
problem. The subject matter was abstruse, and the Greeks had
no word to describe it. The solution was to call the volume
Metaphysics, which means "that which follows physics." The term
stuck and is still widely used today. The word *ontology,* meaning
"the science of being," is often used synonymously with *metaphysics.*
During the Middle Ages, when philosophers gave more attention
to metaphysics than to theory of knowledge, the former was
frequently characterized as "first philosophy" or the "study of
being as such."

One of the many metaphysical problems is exhibited by the
clash between *monism* and *pluralism.* The monist holds that the
totality of what exists constitutes an ordered whole, or a completely
unified system; the pluralist denies that this is true. Probably the
most thoroughly monistic metaphysics was that of Benedict Spinoza,
a Dutch Jewish philosopher of the seventeenth century. Like many
other rationalists, he argued that every event within nature is so
related to every other event that none can be fully understood without a knowledge of its relationships to all others. The best known
pluralists are the American pragmatist philosophers of the late
nineteenth and twentieth centuries. One of them, Charles Peirce,
said that it is ridiculous to suppose that there are events which
cannot be fully understood without our knowing that the mayor
of Hong Kong recently had a sneezing fit. Another pragmatist,
William James, said that it would be truer to regard the universe
as a "blooming, buzzing confusion" than as a completely unified
system.

A second metaphysical problem concerns the relationship between mind and matter, or body and soul. Are mind and matter
two radically different kinds of things? If so, can there be any interaction between them? The American pragmatists have maintained that mental or psychic events are as natural as physical events

and that the bifurcation of reality into mental and physical is completely arbitrary. Others, however, among them Descartes, insisted that the mental and the physical constitute wholly distinct realms of being.

A third metaphysical problem has to do with the existence of God and his relationship to the world. Does God exist? If so, does he dwell in nature or is he separate from nature? Those who argue that God exists and dwells within nature are said to believe in an *immanent* God; those who say that he exists apart from or beyond nature are said to believe in a *transcendent* God. Those who deny God's existence altogether are called *atheists;* while those who believe that the question of God's existence is insoluble are called *agnostics.*

A fourth metaphysical problem concerns the existence and nature of the external world. Positions with respect to this problem range from the view that the external world obviously exists and has those properties the naked senses tell us it has to the view that there is no external physical world and that all reality is mental. The former position is known as *naive realism;* the latter, as *metaphysical idealism.*

Ethical Problems. The third branch of philosophy we shall consider is called *ethics.* A synonym for *ethics* is *morals,* and both words have a similar etymology. *Ethics* derives from the Greek word *ethos,* meaning customs, while *morals* derives from the Latin word *mores,* which also means customs. Once again, however, etymology is an insufficient clue to modern usage or even to the ethical writings of classical philosophers. Among the problems moral philosophers discuss are:

(1) What constitutes human happiness or well-being? One prominent position with respect to this question is known as *hedonism,* which was espoused by, among others, the Greek philosopher Epicurus and the nineteenth-century English philosopher John Stuart Mill. To the hedonist, happiness consists in a life with many pleasures and few pains. Another position, one held by Aristotle, is called *eudemonism.* According to the eudemonist, human well-being consists in the active exercise of one's natural or innate faculties, especially reason, which Aristotle regarded as the sole faculty distin-

guishing man from the beasts. Still a third position is that of Thomas Aquinas and most other Christian philosophers, for whom happiness as defined by hedonists and eudemonists is an inferior grade of human well-being. To enjoy true happiness man must embrace the *theological* (as opposed to the natural) *virtues* of faith, hope, and love and put himself into a proper relationship to God.

(2) What is the relationship between human happiness and right conduct? On this question the principal division is between teleologists and deontologists. *Teleologists,* among them John Stuart Mill, define right conduct as conduct conducive to human well-being. *Deontologists,* on the other hand, take the view that the nature of right conduct can be known without taking into account its possible consequences for human weal or woe. The most famous of the deontologists is the eighteenth-century German philosopher Immanuel Kant, who claimed that it would be wrong to tell a lie even to save another man's life.

(3) What can reason tell us about the nature of right conduct and human happiness? Teleologists usually say that reason can, at least in principle, tell us what kinds of conduct lead to human happiness and to this extent help us decide what acts are right. They do not agree, however, with respect to the competence of reason to determine what constitutes happiness. Some have argued that reason is purely instrumental—that is, it can tell us how to achieve what we *consider* desirable, but it cannot tell us the nature of happiness itself. This must be determined by pure feeling. Deontologists, on the·other hand, often claim that beliefs about right conduct can be justified by rational insight.

(4) What is the individual's moral obligation when conflicts arise between his own and others' interests? One position, known as *egoism,* is that individuals are psychologically compelled to pursue their own interests as they conceive them and that no one can be morally obliged to do the impossible. The opposite position, called *altruism,* is that individuals can and on occasion ought to promote the interests of others even at the cost of their own well-being.

This sampling of philosophical problems is necessarily incomplete and is intended only to suggest some of the typical concerns of philosophy. In addition to those discussed, philosophy has a number of other branches, each with its own particular problems. Among these other branches, to name only a few, are logic, or the study of correct reasoning; esthetics, or the study of art and beauty; the philosophy of religion; the philosophy of education; political philosophy; and legal philosophy.

CRITICAL AND SPECULATIVE PHILOSOPHY

Though much of the confusion regarding the nature of philosophy derives from the extent and variety of its subject matter, considerable confusion also stems from the fact that philosophers approach their subject matter with different intents and by different methods. In these respects the principal division is between critical and speculative philosophizing.

The first great master of critical philosophy was Socrates. He wrote nothing and is best known to us through dialogues written by Plato, who was his disciple and later the teacher of Aristotle. In the Platonic dialogues Socrates is ordinarily cast in the role of an interrogator of other men's views rather than as an expositor of his own ideas. In fact, Plato often has Socrates say that he knows nothing. When one of his disciples reported that an oracle had declared him to be the wisest of all men, Socrates was at first puzzled. Then he realized that, whereas other men believed that they knew much though in fact they knew nothing, he knew nothing and knew that he knew nothing. Many commentators have questioned Socrates' sincerity in claiming to know nothing, and they are no doubt right to do so. Yet this pretense of ignorance, or "Socratic irony," is significant; for Socrates was primarily a teacher, and his pedagogical function, as he saw it, was not to indoctrinate his followers but rather to help them examine their beliefs critically and overcome their prejudices.

Socrates was struck by the fact that, though philosophical matters are weighty and difficult and men seldom give more than a few leisure moments to their study, almost everybody has very decided opinions about them. Carpenters, shoemakers, and shipbuilders, he pointed out, work hard to learn their crafts, and persons who have not served an apprenticeship with a master in one of these crafts do not pretend to a knowledge of them. Yet almost everybody believes that he can say of what happiness consists or what form of government is most desirable. Socrates was even more impressed by the fact that most men's opinions on philosophical matters are highly confused and self-contradictory, despite the confidence with which they are held.

The first step in educating others, therefore, is to expose the immodesty of prejudice, to "purify the soul" of ungrounded beliefs and fuzzy thinking. How well Socrates succeeded in his mission as educator is a moot point. There can be no question that he made a deep impression on his own circle, but to the mass of Athenians he was merely an object of ridicule or resentment, and in the end they executed him for "worshipping false gods and corrupting the young." Socrates had thought that by exposing the murkiness and inconsistency of a man's beliefs he would make the man "angry with himself" and thus "gentler" to others. Usually, however, the anger Socrates aroused was directed against himself.

Perhaps because of Socrates' fate, few philosophers have practiced critical philosophy with his boldness and tenacity. Still, critical philosophy has had a long and distinguished history and is once again in the ascendant. The philosopher, it is often said today, has no responsibility to pronounce on philosophical issues; rather, his job is to clarify philosophical beliefs and to examine them for internal consistency. If he succeeds in expressing precisely and without ambiguity what were previously vague and only half-articulated beliefs and further if he is able to establish the consistency or inconsistency of these beliefs with other related beliefs, then he has done as much as anyone has a right to expect of him in his professional capacity.

Although the flavor and style of critical philosophy as practiced today are very different from what they were in Socrates' day, the basic stratagems for achieving its goals have not greatly altered. One of the most important of these is to clarify the terms in which we couch our beliefs by locating them within the larger family of words to which they belong. In Plato's day this method was called *dialectic*. A simple—though, according to Socrates, not wholly successful —example of dialectic may be found in the dialogue *Laches*, which, like many of the earlier Platonic dialogues, focuses on the analysis of a key term. In this case the key term is courage. The word courage is related to the term virtue since courage is one of the virtues; it is also related, if only indirectly, to the term wisdom since wisdom is also one of the virtues. Furthermore, "courage" is obviously related to "rashness," though in a way which may at first appear obscure. By calling Laches' attention to the interrelationships of these terms, Socrates guides him toward a more satisfactory definition of "courage" than the one that had first occurred to him:

soc. And now, Laches, do you try and tell me . . . what is the common quality which is called courage, and which includes all the various uses of the term . . . .

LA. I should say that courage is a sort of endurance of the soul, if I am to speak of the universal nature which pervades them all.

soc. But that is what we must do if we are to answer the question. And yet I cannot say that every kind of endurance is, in my opinion, to be deemed courage. Hear my reason: I am sure, Laches, that you would consider courage to be a very noble quality.

LA. Most noble, certainly.

soc. And you would say that wise endurance is also good and noble?

LA. Very noble.

soc. But what would you say of a foolish endurance? Is not that, on the other hand, to be regarded as evil and hurtful?

LA. True.

soc. And is anything noble which is evil and hurtful?

LA. I ought not to say that, Socrates.

soc. Then you would not admit that sort of endurance to be courage— for it is not noble, but courage is noble.

LA. You are right.

soc. Then, according to you, only the wise endurance is courage.

LA. True.[1]

Here someone objects that if courage is wise endurance, then beasts without wisdom cannot be courageous. Plato has another character in the dialogue answer this objection:

I do not call animals or any other things which have no fear of dangers, because they are ignorant of them, courageous, but only fearless and senseless. Do you imagine that I should call little children courageous, which fear no dangers because they know none? There is a difference,

---

[1] *The Dialogues of Plato,* trans. Benjamin Jowett (New York: Oxford University Press, 1961), I, 67–68. Reprinted by permission of the publisher.

to my way of thinking, between fearlessness and courage. I am of opinion that thoughtful courage is a quality possessed by very few, but that rashness and boldness, and fearlessness, which has no forethought, are very common qualities possessed by many men, many women, many children, many animals. And you, and men in general, call by the term *courageous* actions which I call rash;—my courageous actions are wise actions.[2]

It is clear that by making our beliefs explicit and expressing them in precise language, we may also succeed in exposing inconsistencies that would otherwise go unnoticed. Consequently, what Plato called dialectic is both a method for clarifying beliefs and a method for discovering inconsistencies among them. Frequently, however, we must supplement this method, for it often happens that two clearly stated propositions appear to be consistent when considered by themselves but can be shown to be inconsistent when viewed in the light of some other relevant but overlooked proposition. To guard against inconsistency, therefore, we must do more than clarify our beliefs; we must also trace their consequences. Suppose, for instance, that we have succeeded in clarifying beliefs A and B, and they appear to be consistent. If, however, on proceeding further we discover that the truth of A implies the truth of C and that the truth of C implies the falsity of B, then we know that A and B are not compatible despite our initial impression.

This general method of exposing inconsistencies by tracing the implications of our beliefs is also abundantly illustrated in Plato's dialogues. In *Euthyphro,* a dialogue devoted to the analysis of piety, for example, the principal interlocutor, Euthyphro, is prosecuting his father for the murder of a slave. He claims to be acting out of piety. In typically ironic fashion Socrates claims to know nothing about the nature of piety and asks Euthyphro to enlighten him. Euthyphro obliges with several definitions of piety, each of which Socrates shows to be unacceptable. The dialogue ends as Euthyphro, claiming the pressure of business, walks off in confusion.

One of the definitions proposed by Euthyphro is this: Acts of piety are those of which the gods approve. To show the inadequacy of this definition Socrates gets Euthyphro to admit that one and the same act cannot be both pious and impious and also that acts

2 *Ibid.,* p. 73.

approved by some of the gods are disapproved by others. He then points out that if Euthyphro's definition were accepted some acts would be both pious and impious.

In brief, then, the goals of critical philosophy are to clarify the beliefs we actually hold and to examine them for internal consistency.

Many philosophers, however, have refused to limit themselves to critical philosophy. They have reached beyond clarity and consistency toward a better understanding of human experience and of the world man inhabits. The world may not be a "blooming, buzzing confusion," as William James suggested, but most philosophers agree that this is the way it appears to our untutored senses; they have often asked whether the world as presented in raw experience does not have greater coherence and order than it seems to have. As Aristotle put it, "philosophy begins in wonder"—a naive, childlike wonder akin to that of the artist who is overawed by the mystery and strangeness of what he sees. Unlike many artists, however, philosophers are not content to record their reaction to the world in its immediacy and concreteness. Rather, they seek to explain the world by devising theoretical concepts and general categories which fit the facts of immediate experience but at the same time satisfy the intellect's demand for order. To this effort we give the name *speculative philosophy*.

In recent years speculative philosophy has been on the wane in England and America. The principal reason is the spectacular success and growing prestige of modern science. It is often said nowadays that more can be learned about nature and human experience through scientific method, with its emphasis on laboratory experiment and mathematical rigor, than through the philosopher's armchair meditations. At the same time there is an increasing suspicion of the speculative philosopher's theoretical concepts and general categories. More and more they are being evaluated according to criteria which scientists have found useful in their own domains and pronounced unsatisfactory. Speculative philosophers usually counter these charges by arguing that science itself rests upon nonscientific assumptions and that despite its great successes in predicting and controlling natural events it has still not established its claim of being the most fundamental account of reality.

Whatever the merits of speculative philosophy, almost all the great classical philosophers have practiced it in one degree or another, and it is still far from being in total eclipse. To ignore it would be to ignore most of the history of philosophy as well as several vigorous twentieth-century philosophical movements such as pragmatism and existentialism. Moreover, many speculative philosophical systems have had a powerful impact upon the popular mind and have influenced, directly or indirectly, the course of world history. Christianity and Marxism, for instance, both incorporate world outlooks that owe a great deal to speculative philosophy. Christianity was greatly influenced by Plato and Aristotle; Marxism, by the German philosopher G. W. F. Hegel, who lived and wrote at the turn of the nineteenth century. Indeed, modern science itself owes a heavy debt to the speculative philosophical atomists of the fourth century B.C.

In Chapter Four we shall discuss the speculative philosophies of Plato and Aristotle at some length. Here let us consider very briefly the atomist and Hegelian systems just mentioned. Atomism is best known to us today through Epicurus, a Greek contemporary of Aristotle, and through Lucretius, a Roman follower of Epicurus. According to them, the ultimate constituents of whatever exists are very tiny objects that cannot be observed by the naked eye. These tiny objects, called atoms, vary in size, shape, and weight. They normally fall through the void, or empty space, perpendicularly in a straight line; but from time to time for no assignable reason some of them swerve, causing collisions and giving rise to clusters of atoms. The objects we know through the physical senses are such clusters of atoms. Their great variety is due to the great variety of atoms themselves and to the almost endless possibilities of combination and recombination. The human soul itself is regarded as a particular constellation of atoms—much finer and smoother than those of physical objects. In waking consciousness, the soul-atoms quiver and dance; in sleep, their activity is subdued; in death, they are dispersed throughout the void.

Hegel believed that the ultimate reality is a single, all-embracing entity which he called the Absolute Spirit. Nature, the entire sweep of history, and the conscious life of all living creatures are but manifestations of the infinite activity of this Absolute Spirit, which unfolds itself in time according to a dynamic and irreversible process. Men, even world-historical figures like Napoleon, may consciously pursue goals which run athwart the goals of the Absolute Spirit. But the Absolute Spirit, more cunning than they, will use even their wrong-headedness to achieve its goals. At times, the movement of the Absolute Spirit results in stages of equilibrium or stability. Such stages, however, inevitably generate reactions which propel the world-process toward more complex and higher stages of evolution. What is most valuable in the earlier stages is retained and reconciled in the higher stages. To understand the workings of the Absolute Spirit we must think in terms of triads: thesis, antithesis, and synthesis. One moment or stage (the thesis) gives rise to its opposite (the antithesis), which in turn is supplanted by a higher stage (the synthesis) that incorporates and harmonizes features of both thesis and antithesis. (This process is called *dialectical,* but the reader must take care not to confuse Hegelian dialectic with Platonic dialectic. As often happens in philosophy, the same word is used in two different senses.)

These descriptions of atomist and Hegelian theories, though sketchy, illustrate three of the more prominent features of speculative philosophy. First, speculative philosophers refuse to accept the world of ordinary experience as ultimate. Atoms and the Absolute Spirit are represented as being in some sense more real than the world as we know it in everyday life. Second, the crucial concepts in speculative philosophy are products of the human mind. They are expected to explain ordinary experience, but they are not directly suggested by it. Nobody has ever seen an atom or actually confronted the Absolute Spirit. Third, speculative philosophical theories are very general. They are intended to explain the whole of reality not some limited part of it. Everything, said Epicurus and Lucretius, is made up of atoms and the void. Everything, said Hegel, is a manifestation of the Absolute Spirit.

PHILOSOPHY AND SCIENCE

Since science has grown out of philosophy and since philosophy has roots in a tradition that includes the beginnings of science, it would be surprising if either could be demarcated sharply from the other. The differences are largely differences of degree, not of kind. It is not, for instance, true as has often been said, that science consists of bodies of knowledge beyond any reasonable doubt, whereas philosophy consists of fanciful speculations for which no evidence may be adduced and whose appeal is solely to feeling or imagination. On the one hand, although particular scientific theories have often elicited widespread assent, many scientists have proposed theories which they themselves admit to be highly speculative. Speculative theorizing is in fact often a necessary prelude to significant scientific discovery. Moreover, even the most solidly based scientific theories are subject to modification or abandonment. Probably no scientific theory enjoyed such widespread and wholehearted approval as did Newtonian physics in the eighteenth century. The German philosopher Kant actually based a good bit of his metaphysics upon the belief that Newtonian physics was indubitably true. Yet several of the fundamental assumptions of Newtonian physics have been abandoned by the scientific community in the twentieth century, and, as Einstein and other scientists have often reminded us, twentieth-century physics itself will no doubt undergo fundamental change in the future.

On the other hand, although speculative philosophical schemes often appeal more strongly to feeling and imagination than do purely scientific theories, speculative philosophers have often tried to support their views with evidence not radically different in kind from what scientists offer in support of their own. The philosophical atomists, for instance, argued for their views by citing observable facts. Sound, they pointed out, travels through walls, but if walls were as solid as they seem this would be impossible. Only, they said, by assuming that walls are composed of atoms with empty space between them can we account for this phenomenon. Similarly, how can we account for the fact that bodies of equal volume should have different densities and weights if we do not assume a difference in atomic structure?

Neither is it true that science is concerned only with observable facts whereas speculative philosophy freely posits the existence of unobservable entities. The truth is that both scientists and philosophers make use of hypothetical entities for whose existence they can offer no direct evidence. Atoms as conceived of in contemporary scientific theory are no more observable than the atoms of classical atomistic philosophy. Even with the most high-powered microscopes they have escaped observation. Of course, contemporary atomic theory is better grounded than classical atomic theory. The point is that in both cases the evidence is indirect. Thus, those who disparage on grounds of scientific inadequacy the philosopher's attempt to establish the existence of unobservable entities are under a serious misapprehension about the nature of science. Still, science and philosophy do each have features permitting us to make a rough and ready distinction.

(1) Philosophers deal with questions that are in some sense more basic or fundamental than those posed by scientists. For instance, scientists generally assume that all events in nature are causally determined and can be explained in terms of natural laws. Scientists also assume that if two types of events have regularly accompanied one another in certain kinds of past situations they will continue to accompany one another in the same kinds of situations in the future. It has been plausibly argued that if either or both of these assumptions were false, science would be seriously undermined. Yet the scientist in his professional capacity does not concern himself with the truth of these assumptions. These fundamental questions fall to the philosopher.

(2) The phenomena studied by scientists are almost invariably measurable. In fact, nothing so thoroughly distinguishes modern science from philosophy as its extensive reliance upon mathematics. Philosophers do not ordinarily give their theories a mathematical formulation.

(3) Scientists frequently employ experimental techniques, actually manipulating aspects of our natural environment to test hypotheses. Philosophers, though often eager to use data obtained by scientific experiment as premises in their own thinking, do not themselves make experiments.

(4) Equally competent scientists who study the same kinds of phenomena very often arrive at identical conclusions, even though their investigations have been conducted independently. By contrast equally competent philosophers working independently on the same problems notoriously tend to come up with different conclusions.

(5) Sometimes scientific discoveries and theories have a bearing on human conduct and are used to justify one course of behavior over another. Scientists as such, however, are not concerned with these implications of their work. Philosophers, on the contrary, rarely theorize without considering the human or moral implications of their thinking. Epicurus and Lucretius, for instance, advanced the atomic theory not only because they thought that it was required to explain observable facts but also because they believed that their view of the nature of the universe would bring consolation to those who feared suffering in an afterlife and would show that in life we ought not to be concerned about the gods.

▟▟

Chapter Two

THE NATURE

AND EXISTENCE

OF THE EXTERNAL WORLD

IN the ordinary conduct of life we are likely to take for granted that there is an external world and that our physical senses bear accurate testimony both to its existence and to its nature. These assumptions are so deeply rooted in our system of beliefs that most of us would regard an unquestioning acceptance of them as a test of sanity. It may, therefore, come as a surprise to learn that the evidence for these beliefs is less than conclusive and that they appear flatly to contradict other beliefs that we hold no less tenaciously. Consider the following points.

(1) All of us at one time or another have had dreams, and a surprisingly large number of persons have had hallucinations. When we are dreaming or hallucinating, we are thoroughly convinced that the content of our experience has an external existence. It appears to be presented to us from the outside; we do not experience it as something produced from within. Moreover, there is no intrinsic mark, nothing in the content of the experience itself, which permits us to distinguish it from an object presented to us through the physical senses in ordinary waking experience. Dream red is no less vivid than real red, nor is a square object any less square simply because it is dreamt. It follows that the mere fact of having an experience of any sensible quality or object cannot be adequate evidence for its existence as an external reality. If the belief in

externally existing objects that accompanies dreams and hallucinations is false and if the intrinsic nature of individual waking sense experiences is like that of individual dream and hallucinatory experiences, the belief that accompanies the waking sense experiences may be equally false.

(2) All of us realize that some of our waking sense experiences mislead us about the true nature of the object experienced. A straight stick half submerged in water looks bent; a square tower viewed from a sufficient distance looks round. When the stick is removed from the water, however, it looks straight, and we conclude that it is in fact straight. When the tower is viewed from a closer vantage point, it looks square, and we take this as evidence that it is square. But the initial sense experiences, considered by themselves, contained nothing that would permit us to infer they were misleading: the half-submerged stick really did look bent; the tower viewed from a distance really did look round. Just as dreams and hallucinations are in and of themselves like waking experiences, so "fallacious" or "misleading" sense experiences in a waking state are in and of themselves like the "veridical" ones. With what right, then, do we make this distinction between fallacious and veridical sense experiences? If some of our waking sense experiences are fallacious even though they do not differ in their intrinsic nature from those called veridical, perhaps *all* waking sense experiences are fallacious.

(3) It is generally agreed that changes in the properties of externally existing physical objects do not depend upon changes in the position of an observer or in his physiological state. Sense experiences, however, do depend upon the position and physiological state of the observer. According to the angle from which a penny is observed, it will appear either round or elliptical. Certain drugs will alter our color perceptions; an object that appears a dull red before the ingestion of these drugs may afterwards appear bright scarlet. Therefore, we are either wrong in believing that sense experience gives us direct and immediate knowledge of physical objects or wrong in believing that the nature of physical objects is independent of the position of the observer and his physiological state.

NAIVE REALISM

The three points just developed tend to refute the position called *naive realism*. Stated briefly, this is the view that physical objects are immediately and directly present to us in sense experience. Naive realism may, however, take two forms, which will here be called simple naive realism and sophisticated naive realism. *Simple naive realism* is the view that a physical object is directly present to us in each and every waking sense experience and that the proof of the object's presence and nature lies in the individual sense experience itself. *Sophisticated naive realism* holds first that physical objects are present to us directly only in some, not all, sense experiences, and second that evidence for the existence and nature of a physical object lies not in the single sense experience itself but rather in the manner in which the individual experience is related to other sense experiences. Against simple naive realism each of the three objections already presented seems to be conclusive. In its sophisticated form, naive realism is less vulnerable.

For the sophisticated naive realist the external world is an aggregate of physical objects related to one another according to laws of nature. In order to determine whether any apparent physical object presented to us in sense experience is a genuine part of the external world, it is necessary and sufficient to determine whether its relationships to other bodies are those demanded by the laws of nature. In dream experience the laws of nature are suspended: unsupported bodies float in midair, flames fail to burn, paintings suddenly come to life. In waking experience the laws of nature remain in full force: unsupported bodies in midair fall to the ground, fires burn, and paintings remain inanimate. This is why the body of our waking experience is veridical whereas dream experiences are not.

As for the "errors of sense" in waking experience, the sophisticated naive realist points out that unless we assumed the actual presence of at least some physical objects to our senses the expression would be completely meaningless. In speaking of a waking sense experience as misleading, we are merely affirming that because of a particular complex of circumstances and in accordance with certain laws of nature *which are themselves knowable only by sense experience* the object shows itself differently than it normally would. Consider again the half-submerged stick that appears bent. Why do we say it is really straight? We do so because, first, we can compare the initial visual observation with the visual and tactile sense experiences we have upon lifting the stick from the water and running our hand along it and because, second, these latter experiences together with other waking sense experiences give evidence for certain laws of nature from which the fact of a straight stick's appearing bent when half-submerged in water can be deduced. If we did not assume the validity of these other sense experiences, we would have not the slightest reason to question the validity of the first.

But how can the sophisticated naive realist reconcile his conviction regarding the direct presence of physical objects in waking experience with the belief that physical objects remain what they are despite changes in the circumstances of sensory or perceptual experience? If physical objects appear to us in their own nature, if they do not depend upon the position or physiological state of the observer, then why are we so often deceived? Square towers ought to appear square regardless of our distance from them. Round pennies ought to appear round regardless of the perspective from which we view them. A dull red ought to appear a dull red regardless of our physiological state.

REPRESENTATIONALISM

The apparently insuperable difficulties presented by naive realism, even in its sophisticated form, have induced many philosophers to adopt a position known as *representationalism*. These philosophers maintain that physical objects are never directly present to us in sense experience. They also maintain that whatever exists must be either physical or mental. From these premises they conclude that the content of sense experience is entirely mental. Among the first and the most important of the representationalists were the rationalist Descartes and the seventeenth-century British empiricist John Locke, both of whom averred that nothing is directly present to the human mind except its own ideas. Sense experiences, they insisted, are as thoroughly mental or psychic as abstract ideas, fancies, dreams, memory images, and emotions, and like them fall into the category of *ideas*. The representationalists recognized, of course, that sense experiences can be distinguished from other ideas, and by calling them "ideas" they did not mean to minimize their uniqueness. The intent was rather to emphasize their status as inner mental realities.

To be sure, in sense experience we seem to have direct access to external physical realities. When we see a mountain, the mountain appears to exist in space rather than in our minds. But this is no less true of objects seen in dreams and hallucinations, which clearly have no existence outside of our own minds. Consequently, we cannot use this seeming externality or "outsideness" of what is presented in sense experience as evidence of genuine externality. It is also undeniable that sense experiences (unlike abstract ideas, memory images, or the fancies of our imagination) are involuntary. We can by an act of will evoke an image of a mountain, whereas what we see upon opening our eyes does not depend upon our will. This property of involuntariness, however, belongs no less to hallucinations and dreams than to sense experience. It too, therefore, must be rejected as evidence of genuine externality. The real mark of sense experience, as opposed to other mental contents, is, as the sophisticated naive realist holds, explicability in terms of natural law. Sense experiences are related to one another according to fixed and knowable patterns; the body of sense experience constitutes an orderly and coherent pattern. Dreams and hallucinations do not fit this orderly pattern, and it is precisely for this reason that we refuse to regard them as genuine sense experiences. The mistake of the sophisticated naive realist was to suppose that this property of orderliness, coherence, or explicability in terms of natural law constitutes evidence for the externality of sense experience. In fact, it is merely a property that distinguishes one set of mental experiences from others.

This property, however, demands explanation, and the core of representationalist theory is first that sense experiences are *caused* by externally existing physical objects, and second that the orderliness and coherence of the body of our sense experiences derive from the orderliness and coherence which obtain in the external world of independently existing physical bodies.

The term representationalism suggests that sense experiences are related to physical realities in the way that mirror-images or portraits are related to their originals. This is not entirely incorrect, but it can be very misleading. In representationalist theory sense experiences do in some respects copy or resemble the physical objects that cause them. But in other respects there is no resemblance at all, and even where resemblance exists it is only approximate. The best analogy for understanding the relationship between a physical object and its representation in the mind is not a mirror-image or portrait and its original but rather a statue and its sculptor or a particular pain and its external cause in nature.

Consider the representationalist position more closely. In sense experience we see such things as mountains, trees, chairs, skunks, and violins. These objects of sense experience have a wide variety of properties or qualities: they have sizes and shapes, usually they have colors, often they have odors, and sometimes they emit sounds. Representationalists make a broad distinction between these properties or qualities: some they call *primary qualities,* others, *secondary qualities.* Representationalists do not always agree among themselves as to which qualities are primary and which secondary. All of them, however, include size and shape among the primary qualities. All of them also include odor, color, and sound among the secondary qualities. The following discussion will, therefore, be limited to an account of the differences between the primary qualities of size and shape, on the one hand, and the secondary qualities of odor, color, and sound, on the other.

According to the representationalists, both primary and secondary qualities as revealed in sense experience are causally produced by externally existing physical objects. But whereas externally existing objects do themselves possess primary qualities and tend to cause sense experiences that roughly duplicate their own primary qualities, they do not possess secondary qualities. Sense experiences of secondary qualities have no counterpart of any kind in physical nature. Although it is natural for us to locate colors, sounds, and odors in the external world of physical objects, this is logically a mistake of the same order as identifying a sculptor with his statue or identifying an actually felt pain with an instrument of torture such as a rack. Moreover, the resemblances between the sense experiences of primary qualities and their counterparts in the external world are themselves far from perfect. Often they are extremely remote. The square tower viewed from a distance is actually square, but in sense experience it appears round.

Though representationalism is at odds with our ordinary, commonsensical naive realism, it has become so familiar to us today through modern science that it no longer seems as fanciful or speculative as it did to many of Descartes' and Locke's contemporaries; and there is probably no better evidence of man's tolerance for inconsistency than the fact that today representationalism and naive realism usually manage to get along with one another in our thinking without causing any serious intellectual discomfort. Most of us are by turns naive realists and representationalists without even being aware of the inconsistency. Once the inconsistency has been made explicit, however, the tendency is to choose representationalism, since that seems to enjoy the sanction of modern science and most of us regard science as superior to common sense. But how good is the evidence for representationalism?

That scientists should find representationalism more congenial than naive realism is not surprising. Among other things, scientists seek a mathematically precise body of knowledge upon which general agreement may be secured. This means that they will tend to select for special study those aspects of reality or human experience which are most easily measured, most widely accessible, and whose nature may be established or confirmed by a variety of independent tests. Nothing better facilitates the achievement of these scientific goals than more or less exclusive concern with primary qualities. There are two reasons for this: first, secondary qualities like smell and color cannot be directly measured; primary qualities like size and shape obviously can. Second, a secondary quality is available to us through a single sense. Colors may be known through the sense of sight alone; odors, uniquely by the sense of smell; sounds, exclusively through the sense of hearing. If we have reason to suspect a malfunctioning of one of these senses there is no possibility of testing its adequacy with a second sense. In contrast, primary qualities (which Aristotle called *common sensibles*), are known to us by more than one sense. Shape and size may be perceived both by the sense of sight and by the sense of touch. This means that the genuineness or adequacy of any perception of primary qualities through one sense may be checked by appeal to another. If the half-submerged stick appears bent to the eye, we may test this visual sense experience by employing the sense of touch. This also means that even a blind man is not without resources for establishing the existence and the nature of an object's primary qualities, these qualities being available to the sense of touch as well as to the sense of sight.

It should also be noted in this connection that the sense of touch is widely regarded as a particularly reliable index of reality. Assume for instance that you see a form in a corner of a room that other persons in the same room claim not to see. To test the reality of this form's existence you could attempt to walk through it. If this were impossible, if the sense of touch attested to the form's having size and shape, you would insist upon its reality despite the negative testimony of other persons. Assume now that you are in a room with other people who claim to see a form you cannot see yourself. If once more you employed the test of touch, if again you walked over to the corner and found that the area the form was said to occupy could not be traversed, you would conclude that the form exists despite the negative testimony of your own sense of sight.

But do any of these facts support representationalism? The fact that common sense regards perceptual experiences of primary qualities, especially tactile experiences, as particularly strong evidence for the independent existence of physical objects does not support it. From this fact alone one cannot infer either that physical objects lack secondary qualities or that perceptual experiences of primary qualities are caused by independently existing external objects. The representationalist holds that all perceptual experiences, including those of primary qualities known by touch, are mental events caused by physical realities that are themselves unperceived. To say that we commonly regard perceptual experiences of whatever kind as evidence for the existence of such realities is not to offer evidence for the theory but merely to register agreement with it.

Similarly, the fact that primary qualities are more amenable to mathematical treatment and offer greater possibilities for interpersonal and intersensory confirmation does not prove that any perceptual experience is a purely mental event caused by an independently existing physical reality possessing none but primary qualities. All it shows is that primary qualities, whether they be construed as qualities of sense experience or qualities of physical realities, have a special importance for science.

One of the most carefully worked out philosophical arguments on behalf of representationalism is Descartes', though it rests upon assumptions which few persons would defend today. Following is the argument stated in summary form:

(1) God exists.
(2) God is by definition a benevolent being.
(3) A benevolent God will necessarily give to man a faculty by which he can with proper effort understand the world.
(4) This God-given faculty by which man can understand the world is reason.
(5) The criterion by which we decide whether the faculty of reason has been properly used is the clarity and distinctness of the ideas it produces.
(6) Whatever can be clearly and distinctly understood must exist.
(7) Whatever can be understood mathematically can be clearly and distinctly understood.
(8) An external world having none but primary qualities is susceptible to mathematical analysis and can consequently be clearly and distinctly understood.

∴ An external world having none but primary qualities exists.

Although the argument as stated is original with Descartes, the gist of it can be found in the writings of such seventeenth-century scientists as Kepler and Galileo, who construed God as a master

mathematician and therefore regarded mathematics as "the language of the world."

Descartes' rationalism is evident in his proof of representationalism. It must not be thought, however, that representationalism
is an exclusively rationalistic doctrine. It has also been maintained
by empiricists, notwithstanding the fact that they have had far
greater difficulty than the rationalists in justifying it. John Locke,
for instance, accepted in typical empiricist fashion the view that
any knowledge of external physical realities must be derived from
sense experience. Since, however, for Locke, as for all representationalists, sense experience consists entirely of ideas, it is difficult
to see how he could establish the existence of physical objects, and
it is even more difficult to see how he could ever establish their
exact nature and their relationship to sense experience. How,
for example, would Locke ever be able to establish that the
primary qualities of sense experience resemble primary qualities
of externally existing physical realities? If empiricism is a correct
theory of knowledge, the comparison can be made only if we have
sensory experience of externally existing physical realities; but, if
representationalism is metaphysically correct, sense experience of
external realities is impossible because, as Locke says, the mind
"perceives nothing but its own ideas." Though Locke was aware
of this problem, there is general agreement that neither he nor
any other empiricist has provided a satisfactory answer to it.

These last remarks must not be interpreted to mean that representationalism poses no problem for a rationalist like Descartes.
In some limited respects our ideas are copies of physical objects,
but, as we have already seen, the fundamental relationship is a
causal one. The questions thus arise: How can a physical object
cause an idea? How can the material or corporeal give rise to the
mental or spiritual?

To understand this problem we must first consider the term
substance, a term which has played an important role in the history
of philosophy. Like many crucial philosophical terms it has more
than one meaning. In one of its usages *substance* designates that
which exists in its own right, depending for its existence upon
itself alone. According to Descartes, there is, strictly speaking, only
one substance in this meaning of the term—God. However, it is

Descartes' contention that mind—or "thinking substance"—and the external world—or "extended substance"—must also be considered substances in this sense since apart from God they too are self-subsistent. Descartes referred to them collectively as "created substances."

In a second usage *substance* designates an unobservable underlying principle of unity in a being that guarantees this being's essential identity throughout change. Many philosophers, especially Hume, reject this concept; they argue that an individual being is nothing more than a bundle or collection of observable properties or activities. But Descartes and others have maintained that any being is necessarily more than the sum of its observable properties or activities. The mind, for instance, *has* ideas, but it is not identical with the succession of its ideas. Similarly, physical objects *have* properties, but in order to have properties they must first be. And since the properties of an object may change drastically during the course of its existence without the object's ceasing to be what it is, there must be some underlying substratum to which the properties belong and which accounts for the object's continuing identity.

When Descartes speaks of extended substance and thinking substance, the term substance carries both meanings. It is, however, the first of these meanings which is most directly relevant to our present problem. By construing matter and mind as created substances Descartes obviously implied that each constitutes a radically different and independent realm of reality, but it is difficult to see how two radically different and independent types of being could interact. A causal relationship does not necessarily presuppose resemblance between cause and effect; but in order to speak of cause and effect the events or objects involved must at least belong to the same system of reality, and this is what Descartes seems to deny to mind and matter when he classifies them as created substances. The external world consists of physical objects existing in space, and the relationships between these objects are to be understood in terms of mathematical laws. Mind, however, is the arena of ideas, and the principles which govern the succession of ideas are not comprehensible mathematically.

Although Descartes struggled with this problem, even his most fervent admirers were unsatisfied with his attempts to solve it. Several adopted a view known as *occasionalism,* according to which each apparent interaction of mind and matter was a result of direct divine intervention. On the occasion of certain physical events, God would implant in our minds a corresponding idea; interaction between mind and matter in the proper sense of the term interaction is nonexistent.

METAPHYSICAL IDEALISM

As we have seen, John Locke took over Descartes' metaphysical views with respect to the nature of the external world and its relation to the human mind without major change, even though these views presented special difficulties for an empiricist. The second of the great British empiricists, Bishop George Berkeley, flatly rejected them—but not in favor of naive realism, which he rejected no less emphatically. His own position was that all reality is mental; there simply is no independently existing external physical world. This position has been called both *metaphysical idealism* and *subjective idealism.* Since their position has neither the sanction of common sense, as does naive realism, nor the sanction of science, as does representationalism, metaphysical idealists have often been eyed very suspiciously by the philosophically untutored.

Like Descartes and Locke, Berkeley accepted the representationalist contention that whatever is immediately present to the mind, including what is present to the mind in sense experience, is wholly mental. He also agreed with Descartes and Locke that the pattern of our sensory experience (as opposed to dreams, fancies, hallucinations, and other mental contents) constitutes an orderly and coherent system and that this can be plausibly explained only by assuming an external cause. In opposition to Locke, however, he argues: (1) that even if there were a physical world, it would be impossible to prove it; (2) that the representationalist's concept of the physical world is unclear and self-contradictory; and (3) that the special features of sense experience that led Locke to posit the existence of a physical world can be satisfactorily explained as a direct product of divine agency.

(1) Berkeley's argument for the impossibility of proving the existence of a physical world is based on the empiricist contention that the only way in which such knowledge could possibly be acquired is through sense experience, together with the contention that the content of sense experience is entirely mental. The argument itself was presented on page 28; and, as we know, Locke was not unaware of it or of its force. Whereas, however, Locke thought that somehow he could get around this difficulty, Berkeley regarded the argument as conclusive. He was especially scornful of the concept of an underlying material substratum that supports primary qualities but cannot itself be characterized in terms of sensory qualities of any kind. For Berkeley this is a meaningless concept. It should have no place in any genuine empiricist philosophy.

(2) Berkeley's case for the unclarity of the representationalist concept of the physical world rests upon a number of acute and subtle observations. One of them has to do with the nature of primary qualities. The primary qualities, it was maintained, can be known by both the sense of sight and the sense of touch. But, notes Berkeley, the primary quality of shape as known by the sense of sight is *not* the same as the primary quality of shape as known by the sense of touch. A man born blind learns to distinguish shapes by touch; but if he should suddenly acquire the sense of sight, he could not by the sense of sight alone distinguish one shape from another. If immediately after gaining his vision he were presented with a round object and a square object, he could not tell which was which unless he were permitted to touch them. If, then, the tactile sensation of shape is different from the visual sensation of shape, which of these two different sensations is the copy or representation of the primary quality that presumably characterizes independently existing physical objects? To this question representationalists had no ready answer, as Locke, who anticipated this criticism, candidly admitted.

Berkeley's principal argument against the representationalist account of the external world, however, was that it contradicts itself. According to representationalism, the primary qualities of sense experience resemble the primary qualities of physical objects. But, said Berkeley, if the primary qualities of physical objects resemble the primary qualities of sense experience, then the primary qualities of phvsical objects must themselves be ideas, for nothing but an idea can possibly resemble an idea. If the primary qualities of physical objects resemble the primary qualities of sense experience, they must at least belong to the same order of reality. By assuming the truth of representationalism and tracing its consequences, we thus find that the doctrine denies itself.

As just stated, Berkeley's argument suggests that the relationship between sense experience and external reality in representationalist theory is primarily one of resemblance. But the argument may be used with only slight alterations even when the relationship between physical objects and sense experiences is construed more fundamentally in causal terms. As Berkeley in common with many of Descartes' own followers claimed, a brute, inert material being could not conceivably cause a mental or spiritual event such as sense experience.

(3) For Descartes and Locke the physical world is a divine creation. Moreover, as Christians they presumably believed that God created the physical world to serve man's needs and to enhance the quality of man's experience as a spiritual being. But why, asked Berkeley, should God choose this method of achieving his goals? Certainly it is within the power of an infinite and all-powerful being to act directly upon man without the intermediary of a physical world, and it seemed to Berkeley that a spiritual being like God would not stoop so low as to create a physical world of brute matter.

For those who do not believe in God, Berkeley's position will, of course, have no appeal. Even theists may well ask whether his denial of the existence of a physical world is consonant with orthodox Christian doctrine or biblical authority. Moreover, Berkeley's doctrine appears to deny the permanent or continuous reality of what we popularly call physical objects. *Esse est percipii,* or "to be is to be perceived," constitutes a cornerstone of his philosophy. This seems to mean that mountains, trees, and other physical objects have no existence except when they are being perceived (by man or by God). Finally, one may wonder whether the premises Berkeley used to deny the existence of extended or material substances do not also entail a denial of spiritual substance. According to Berkeley's successor in the empiricist tradition, David Hume, we have no direct knowledge of the existence of spirit or soul—not even the finite spirit of individual human beings, much less the infinite spirit of God. When one examines most attentively the contents of one's mind, all that one discovers are ideas; one never encounters a substratum or permanent principle of identity to which these ideas are somehow attached. If, therefore, Berkeley's arguments against the concept of extended substance are valid, he ought consistently to deny the existence of spiritual or thinking substance.

PHENOMENALISM

Representationalism and metaphysical idealism are the great classical positions with respect to the problems of the nature and existence of the external world. More recently a number of philosophers have approached these problems in a radically new way. Their solution is called *phenomenalism*. The premise common to all phenomenalists is that what is immediately present in sense experience cannot properly be characterized as either mental or physical. The root of the difficulties with naive realism, representationalism, and metaphysical idealism is the unwarranted assumption in each case that whatever exists must be either mental or physical.

Since naive realism, which is based on the assumption that the content of sense experience is physical, leads to evident contradictions, this assumption must be false. And since representationalism and metaphysical idealism, which are based on the assumption that the content of sense experience is mental, lead to equally serious difficulties, this second interpretation of sense experience must also be false. Moreover, most phenomenalists are empiricists, and they point out that given an empiricist theory of knowledge the logical consequence of construing sense experience as entirely mental leads logically to an even greater difficulty than any yet suggested. If, they say, all that a man may know or experience is his own ideas, then it is not only impossible to prove the existence of an external world but it is also impossible to prove the existence of other minds. Any one individual's ideas of others will be ideas in his own mind, and the deductive leap from one individual's *ideas* of another person to the *existence* of another person is as unwarranted as that from an idea of a physical object to the existence of the object. Each of us would be imprisoned in his own private subjectivity. If a man chose to maintain that physical objects and other persons exist only as ideas in his mind, no one could refute him. (This position is known as *solipsism*.)

Phenomenalism has assumed many forms, most of them highly technical. Here we shall limit our discussion to a very brief outline of phenomenalism as developed by one contemporary philosopher, A. J. Ayer. Ayer employs the term *sense data* (also *sense contents*) very broadly to include all those things Descartes included under the term idea—not only experiences of the so-called outer world but also internal experiences such as feelings, dreams, hallucinations, and fancies. Ayer's purpose in using the new term is to substitute for "ideas," which suggests something mental, a neutral term that connotes neither mental nor physical reality. According to Ayer these neutral sense data are the ultimate units of experience and the only units which could reasonably be said to be "given" in experience. From the fact that neither the physical nor the mental is directly given to us in experience it does not follow, however, that the mental and the physical are substantial beings lying beyond experience. Ayer is adamant in his insistence that all knowledge is based upon experience and that no knowledge can transcend experience. Thinking substance and extended substance are equally illegitimate concepts. But if mind and matter are not substantial entities, what are they? Ayer's answer is that they are *logical constructs* out of sense data. Minds or souls are nothing other than sets of actual or possible sense data with distinctive characters and special relationships to one another. Similarly, physical objects are merely sets of actual or possible sense data with distinctive qualitative features and relationships of their own. If, of course, minds and physical objects are merely sets of actual or possible sense data, then any statement about a mind or a physical object is, at least in principle, fully translatable into a set of statements about sense data alone. And since Ayer, in common with many other twentieth-century philosophers, prefers to approach philosophical issues through a study of language, this is what he wishes to be understood as saying when he claims that minds and physical objects are logical constructs out of sense data.

The use of the expression "actual or possible" sense data in the foregoing exposition of phenomenalism is significant. Ayer does not contend that physical objects are sets of actual sense data alone. He wishes to do justice to the common-sense conviction that physical objects continue to exist even when there is no experience of the sense data out of which they are constructed. Sentences of the form "x exists even when not observed" (x standing for a physical object) he interprets to mean roughly: "If I or somebody else did such and such things, I or he would experience such and such sense data." For instance, when it is said that there is a desk in an unoccupied room, this could mean that if I or anybody else with normal vision went into the room and looked, we would experience sense data of the kind normally associated with desks. Such unexperienced but possible sense data constitute a part of the meaning of any statement about physical objects.

Although phenomenalism is an attractive theory which successfully avoids the pitfalls of the traditional theories discussed, it is not without difficulties of its own. In the first place, phenomenalists accord that the number of sense-data statements required adequately to translate a statement about a physical object would be very large; and many persons find it odd that the meaning of an apparently simple object-statement such as "There is a desk in the unoccupied room next door" could be as complex as it turns out to be when analyzed by a phenomenalist. In the second place, many philosophers have seriously questioned even the possibility of translating object statements into none but sense-data statements. If, for instance, one says "The desk is ten feet from the wall," one is obviously asserting the existence of a spatial relationship between the desk and the wall. But if sense data are not themselves spatially related to one another, how can one adequately translate the meaning of that statement into a set of statements about sense data alone? If, on the other hand, sense data are related to one another spatially, then must one not grant that at least some sense data are themselves physical objects? Is it not true by definition that any thing locatable in space is a physical object?

⊡⊡

Chapter Three

SOME

REPRESENTATIVE

THEORIES OF KNOWLEDGE

THE discussion in Chapter Two illustrates Socrates' conviction that many popular views on philosophical issues are confused and self-contradictory. It also reveals how the critical attempt to clarify and to expose the inconsistencies of popular thinking leads naturally to a speculative endeavor. If we see that naive realism is self-contradictory and therefore false, we are almost inevitably led to pose questions about the external world and man's relationship to it that take us well beyond common sense. The reader will also have observed how the specific answers given to the essentially metaphysical questions raised in the last chapter depend in great measure upon the philosopher's epistemology, or theory of knowledge. In this chapter—which is devoted primarily to epistemological problems—the inadequacy of common sense, the blend of critical and speculative philosophizing, and the close relationship between epistemology and metaphysics will once again be in evidence.

CARTESIAN RATIONALISM

As noted in Chapter One, the rationalist and the empiricist stress reason or sense experience respectively as the principal ground of knowledge. It will also be recalled that with few exceptions rationalists tend to be more optimistic than empiricists with respect to the scope and reliability of possible human knowledge. Moreover, rationalists tend to be greatly impressed by mathematics and to take it as the model of all genuine knowledge. These generalizations apply to the greatest of the rationalists in the historical tradition: Plato, Descartes, Spinoza, and the seventeenth-century German philosopher Leibniz. Plato was greatly influenced by a school of philosophers known as Pythagoreans, who held that "all things are numbers." Descartes shared with Kepler the conviction that it was a tribute to God to conceive of him as a master mathematician. Spinoza's most famous work, *Ethics,* is written in the manner of a treatise on Euclidean geometry; he begins by stating definitions and axioms from which he claims to deduce theorems. And Leibniz, a contemporary of Spinoza, once predicted that a day would come when instead of arguing with one another, men would simply "sit down and calculate."

In referring to knowledge that may be validated entirely by reason, it has become customary to employ the term *a priori.* Knowledge which requires validation either wholly or in part by sense experience is referred to as *empirical knowledge,* or *a posteriori knowledge.* A priori knowledge is subdivided into two species. The first, which is acquired directly or immediately by pure rational insight, is said to be *intuitive,* or *self-evident.* Examples of intuitive or self-evident a priori propositions are: "The whole is greater than any of its parts"—a familiar geometrical principle—and "Either John is in the library or John is not in the library"—an example of an elementary principle of logic, stating that a proposition must be either true or false. That both sample propositions are a priori follows from the fact that they are known to be true by reason alone. If we know the meanings of the concepts involved and understand the logical structure of the two propositions, we necessarily know that they are true. It is not at all required that we examine any wholes or parts as given in sense experience or that we determine by empirical inquiry where John actually is. That the propositions are intuitively, or self-evidently, true follows from the fact that the truth of each may be recognized by a single act of rational insight. Their truth need *not* be certified by a process of inference or deduction; it is seen or understood in a flash, so to speak. The second species of a priori knowledge is called *demonstrative*. A demonstrative proposition is one whose validity can be determined only by a process of logical or mathematical deduction. Some demonstrative truths follow directly from self-evident truths; others follow only indirectly through the intermediary of other demonstrative truths. The most familiar examples of demonstrative truths are the theorems of Euclidean geometry.

With a very few exceptions, the most notable being the nineteenth-century English philosopher John Stuart Mill, empiricists have not denied that logic and mathematics are a priori bodies of knowledge consisting of none but intuitively or demonstratively true propositions. Neither have they contested that the truths of mathematics and logic are certain or necessary. Finally, empiricists do not deny that logic and mathematics are useful and in some cases even indispensable tools for acquiring, validating, and communicating empirical knowledge. These are not the issues which divide empiricists from rationalists. Rather, the issues are these: (1) Do mathematics and logic by themselves and without the aid of sense experience ever yield reliable knowledge of matters of fact? (2) Are there intuited or demonstrative truths of a nonmathematical or nonlogical character which by themselves yield reliable knowledge of matters of fact? To qualify as a rationalist it suffices to answer "yes" to at least one of these questions, though a typical rationalist answers both affirmatively. To *justify* one's rationalism, however, it is necessary to give a criterion by which one can identify intuitive or self-evident truths and to present actual instances of intuitive or demonstrative truths which do in fact constitute knowledge of genuine matters of fact. Since on these crucial issues of justification, rationalists often fail to agree, generalization beyond this point would be misleading. We shall instead examine here the answers given by the first of the great modern rationalists, René Descartes.

Like many others who have struggled with the problem of self-evidence, Descartes tended to take as his models of self-evident truths elementary propositions in geometry and logic such as the illustrative examples given above. What Descartes apparently did was to inspect these paradigmatic and relatively uncontroversial cases of self-evident knowledge for common traits or characteristics.

Having discovered two such traits, he employed them as criteria in deciding whether other, less typical or more controversial, instances of knowledge could qualify as self-evident. The first of these common traits was indubitability. One cannot easily succeed in doubting that the whole is greater than any of its parts or that a proposition must be either true or false. The second common characteristic was "clarity and distinctness."

Descartes did not explicitly state whether in order to qualify as a self-evident truth a proposition must have both these characteristics or whether one is sufficient. Moreover, he appears to have employed a stronger and a weaker criterion of indubitability. Early in his career he came to the conclusion that most of the basic premises of his thinking, whose truth he had previously taken for granted, were in fact highly questionable. Except for mathematics, which he was convinced rested on solid foundations, he considered the actual bases for what passed as knowledge no more solid than quicksand. Descartes therefore decided to suspend temporarily his beliefs wherever possible and to engage in a systematic and thoroughgoing program of doubt. As a result, he acquired a strong suspicion of sense experience and of naive realism, the grounds of this suspicion being those we discussed in Chapter Two. And although he pointed out that not even a madman or a man in a state of sleep actually questions the self-evident truths of logic and mathematics, he made the point, surprisingly enough, that if we assumed the existence of a very powerful evil spirit (*malin génie*) intent upon deceiving us, we could doubt these truths as well. In fact, he said, if we assume the existence of this evil spirit, there is only one indubitable truth, viz.: "I think; therefore, I am" (*cogito, ergo sum*). The sole thing that even a powerful evil spirit cannot cause me to doubt is that if I am doubting then I must exist.

This is surprising for the following reason. It was Descartes' obvious intent to seek a body of self-evident propositions from which it would be possible to derive certain knowledge about external reality. If, however, self-evident propositions must be indubitable and if the only indubitable proposition is "I think; therefore, I am," Descartes could not conceivably achieve his goal: from the knowledge of one's own existence alone it is manifestly impossible to derive significant knowledge of any other reality.

Descartes later offered a proof of the existence of a benevolent deity who would not tolerate the existence of an evil spirit capable of deceiving us with respect to matters which we clearly and distinctly conceive. But, as has been often pointed out and as will be presently seen, this proof is not derived from "I think; therefore, I am." It follows that if Descartes really believed that all self-evident propositions must be indubitable and that "I think; therefore, I am" is the only indubitable proposition, skepticism with regard to the self-evidence of mathematical and logical truths cannot be rationally overcome.

The fact is, of course, that Descartes did not really doubt the truth of mathematics and logic and that in the elaboration of his philosophical system he freely employed these truths as well as others which he considered equally indubitable or equally clear and distinct. To understand his philosophy, we must therefore assume that its rock bottom consists of not the single absolutely indubitable proposition "I think; therefore, I am," but rather a whole body of propositions that are indubitable in some less exacting sense or that qualify as intuitive truths by virtue of their clarity and distinctness alone.

Another often noted weakness in Descartes' philosophy is a failure to offer a definition of clarity and distinctness. Ideas which seem clear and distinct to some persons will appear vague or ambiguous to others, and even the same person at different times will hold different opinions about the clarity and distinctness of any given idea. For a long time the postulate of Euclidean geometry according to which two parallel lines extended indefinitely would never meet was generally considered perfectly clear and distinct. Yet, the development of non-Euclidean geometries in the nineteenth century and the consequent development of the relativity theory in physics were possible only because some mathematicians found this Euclidean postulate in need of further clarification.

Descartes' "I think; therefore, I am" is itself a proposition whose clarity and distinctness may be called into question. For Descartes, the term *I* in this proposition signified a substantial soul or thinking substance. But many philosophers have argued that the mere existence of a mental state like doubt does not imply the existence of a substantial being. A particular doubt no more testifies to the existence of a thinking substance than the physical event of rain testifies to the existence of a rain substance. And just as the perception of rain is most properly expressed by saying "It is raining," rather than "The rain substance rains," so the most proper way of expressing the fact of doubt is by saying "There is a doubt" rather than "I doubt."

With these comments about Descartes' criteria for identifying self-evident truths in mind, we shall examine a famous Cartesian argument for the existence of God. This argument is presented as an actual instance of an attempted a priori proof of a matter of fact. The proof, freely stated, runs as follows:

(1) I have an idea of God (i.e., of an infinite and perfect being).
(2) All things, including my idea of God, must have a cause.
(3) The only conceivable causes of my idea of God are: (a) myself, (b) the external world, or (c) God himself.
(4) The cause must be at least as great as the effect.
(5) I and the external world, being both finite and imperfect, are less great than my idea of God.

∴ God must be the cause of my idea of God.

∴ God exists.

With regard to this argument several questions might be asked. The one that first comes to mind—namely, is it acceptable?—is not, however, germane to our present discussion. We are not asking whether God's existence may be proven; our interest here is in determining whether a priori proofs of matters of fact are possible. It could be that the argument is acceptable as a proof of God's existence but not acceptable as an instance of an a priori proof of a matter of fact. This would be the case if all the premises were in fact true, but one of them failed to be true a priori. A second question—are all the premises a priori?—is relevant to our present discussion, but it cannot be answered unless we have a criterion for identifying a priori truths, and it must not be uncritically assumed that Descartes' criteria are satisfactory. The crucial question, therefore, is this: are the premises of this argument either self-evident truths or deductions from self-evident truths according to Descartes' own criteria of self-evidence (indubitability and/or clarity and distinctness)?

Is the first premise (I have an idea of God) either indubitable or clear and distinct? It appears not. If by God one means an infinite and perfect being, then the concept of God is no clearer than the concepts of infinity and perfection, both of which are enormously difficult to analyze. Moreover, many persons, including theologians, have argued that a finite and imperfect being like man could not possibly have a clear idea of an infinite and perfect being.

The second premise (All things, including my idea of God, must have a cause) is one that many persons have in fact questioned, and it is doubtful whether the concept of cause, which has given rise to diverse interpretations by philosophers and scientists, is especially clear or distinct.

Similar remarks are in order with respect to the fourth premise which asserts that the cause must be at least as great as the effect. What does this mean? Must the cause be physically as great or spiritually as great? If physically, does this mean in weight, in volume, or in some third sense? If spiritually, does this mean in terms of power, goodness, or some other spiritual property? And regardless of how this premise is interpreted, why should it be accepted as true? Is the flame of a lighted match carelessly tossed from a car as great as the forest fire it causes?

And even if the cause must be as great as its effects, why should my idea of God not be caused by a finite being such as myself or the external world? The implication of the argument seems to be that if God is infinite and perfect then my idea of God must itself be infinite and perfect. No idea, however, conceived as a mental occurrence, can be plausibly construed as infinite or perfect. Ideas come and go, and they are rarely altogether adequate to an understanding of their objects. Descartes tried to get around this difficulty by making a distinction between the material idea—the finite idea existing from time to time in my mind—and the objective idea— apparently the essence of that which the finite idea thinks. But this distinction is far from clear and distinct; and in any case it appears that if the first premise is to be construed as indubitable, it is the material, not the objective, idea which is in question.

The fact that Descartes failed to prove the existence of God from a set of premises each of which is either indubitable or clear and distinct does not itself prove that a priori proofs of matters of real existence are impossible. Yet, Descartes' failure is not without significance. He was, after all, one of the most acute of the rationalists, and his proof of the existence of God is crucial to his entire system. Even his proof of the external world, presented in Chapter Two, presupposes God's existence.

CLASSICAL EMPIRICISM

It is customary to use the label *empiricist* in referring, among others, to the ancient Greek philosopher Aristotle, to the medieval philosopher St. Thomas Aquinas, and to the trio of modern British philosophers Locke, Berkeley, and Hume. Generalizations about these traditional empiricist thinkers are even more hazardous than generalizations about the traditional rationalists. In fact, the term *empiricist* is so vague that there is a serious question as to whether it properly applies to Aristotle and St. Thomas at all, and even Locke's claim to the title has been disputed.

Although all genuinely empiricist thinkers attach relatively more importance to sense experience than to reason, there are two different roles which sense experience may be held to play. On the one hand, sense experience may be seen as the principal or unique *source* of our ideas. "Nothing," said St. Thomas, "is in the intellect which was not first in the senses." On the other hand, sense experience may be regarded as a necessary condition for confirming or establishing the truth of our ideas about matters of fact, regardless of where these ideas may have originated. These two ways of regarding sense experience are distinct; and although Locke, Berkeley, and Hume believed that sense experience played both roles and often failed to distinguish clearly between them, it is possible to be an empiricist in one sense without being an empiricist in the other. Actually, Aristotle and St. Thomas may be considered empiricists only in the first sense, and largely for this reason many philosophers are reluctant to use the term in referring to them.

This reluctance is especially common among contemporary empiricists, who most often prefer a definition of empiricism in the second sense. Nonetheless, the issues posed by these two senses of the term are not unrelated, especially in the form in which they were considered by the classical British empiricists; and it is best for our purposes to use the word in its wide meaning.

In the early modern period empiricism as a theory about the origin of our ideas contrasts with and may even be regarded as an extended polemic against what is known as the theory of innate ideas. This latter theory is attributed most notably to Descartes. Its essence is that God implants in the human mind at birth a set of ideas of which we may become actively aware by the use of reason alone. The empiricist counterclaim is that all ideas derive from experience. In the words of Locke, the mind is at birth like a blank sheet of paper (a *tabula rasa*) upon which experience alone may make an imprint. In another metaphor, Locke refers to the mind at birth as an empty cabinet which comes later to be stocked with none but materials provided by experience. In order to deal seriously with these issues, we will have to determine what the empiricists have in mind when they say: "All *ideas* derive from *experience*." None has given us a fully clear definition of either term, and the various parties to the dispute have employed different vocabularies in trying to elucidate these concepts. To help clarify the issues, we shall substitute the term *sensation*—either external or internal—for the term experience in the following discussion. By *external sensations* we shall mean shapes, colors, and all other qualities known by the aid of the physical senses. By *internal sensations* we shall mean such things as pleasure, pain, jealousy, joy, fear, and all other primary experiences known by introspection rather than by the physical senses. For the term ideas we shall substitute the two terms *images* and *concepts,* the former to mean whatever may be present to the imagination. The term *concepts* will be explained later.

It should be immediately observed that believers in innate ideas do not deny that images derive from sensation. If a man is born blind and has never experienced the sensation of blue, he cannot have an image of blue. Similarly, if a man has never had the sensation of pain, he will not be able to imagine it. It is simply beyond

the power of the imagination to conjure up the image of a particular sensation which has never actually been experienced, although the imagination is free to unite sensations in a complex
image to represent objects which have never actually been experienced and which may even never have existed. For instance, the
imagination may evoke an image of a winged horse, but the qualities out of which this complex image is constituted must all have
been sensed at some time in order for this to be possible. (Hume
pointed out possible exceptions to this generalization. If, he said,
a man had had sensations of several shades of a given color and
were to try to visualize an intermediary shade which he had never
actually sensed, he could probably succeed. Hume contended, however, that exceptions like these are rare and in any case fail to
support the doctrine of innate ideas.)

The issues, then, dividing those who argue that all ideas derive
from experience and those who insist on the existence of innate
ideas concern the status of what we earlier referred to as concepts
and the kind of meaning, if any, which attaches to the words re-
putedly used to express concepts. But what are concepts? Stated
briefly, a concept is any mental content which is neither a sensation nor an image. As an example of a concept Descartes offered
the notion of a thousand-sided figure. If, he said, one failed to
make a careful distinction between images and concepts, one could
easily be led to believe that the term thousand-sided figure stood
for an image and that the image of a thousand-sided figure ex-
hausted the meaning of the term. But this is a serious mistake.
The term thousand-sided figure is very precise, whereas the image
of a thousand-sided figure is extremely vague. When one tries to
picture a thousand-sided figure the image which comes to mind is
something shadowy which hardly differs at all from an image of a
hundred-sided figure. The term thousand-sided figure must, therefore, express some mental content that is more precise and thus
different from the image of a thousand-sided figure. That mental
content is a concept.

Another example of a concept would be the notion of a triangle.
All sensed triangles are either right triangles, isosceles triangles, or
equilateral triangles, and whenever one tries to picture a triangle
the image evoked will be one of these three specific figures. But the

word triangle refers equally to all of them. The word must therefore stand for a concept as opposed to an image, since any image the word evokes is invariably too specific to carry the meaning of this abstract and general term.

As these examples illustrate, concepts are not only different from images and sensations, they are also, at least at times, more clear and distinct. It is, therefore, understandable that in view of Descartes' rationalistic bent, he regarded concepts as innate ideas rather than products of sense experience. In fact, even without an antecedent rationalistic bias it would be plausible to regard concepts as innate ideas; for if it is granted that concepts are or may be more clear and precise than sensations or images, it is difficult to see how they could be derived from the latter.

One empiricist rejoinder to Descartes and other believers in innate ideas is simply to deny the existence of concepts. But this poses a problem. Descartes had assumed, and the classical empiricists agreed, that all meaningful words must stand for or represent ideas. If, therefore, there is no concept of, say, a thousand-sided figure or a triangle in general, it would seem to follow that the terms thousand-sided figure and triangle are meaningless. Locke, Berkeley, and Hume each struggled with this problem in his own way, but probably the clearest answer is Berkeley's. Berkeley said that although terms are meaningful only if they stand for ideas, it is not necessary that they stand for ideas as precise in meaning as the terms themselves. If, for instance, the term triangle is to be meaningful, we must be able to visualize or imagine triangles, but it is not necessary that any or every image have precisely those properties and only those properties connoted by the term triangle. Indeed, if this were necessary, how could we explain the ability of a geometry teacher to communicate the meaning of "triangle" to his students by drawing a far from perfect triangle on the blackboard? Meaningful terms, which believers in innate ideas say stand for concepts, in reality stand for images. The fact that no one image precisely duplicates the meaning of the term for which it stands does not justify the inference that there exists a class of ideas different from and superior to images.

Berkeley's answer to believers in innate ideas is not wholly satisfactory. His account of the meaning of geometrical terms like thousand-sided figure and triangle is, perhaps, acceptable, but it cannot be generalized to cover the whole body of mathematical and logical terms. Thousand-sided figure and triangle are terms denoting empirical realities that can be sensed and consequently imagined. But what about the mathematical term zero or the logical term none? These expressions do not seem to stand for any sensible object; and since what cannot be sensed cannot be imagined, there can be no images of any kind corresponding to them. If, therefore, Descartes and Berkeley are right in their fundamental and common assumption that terms are meaningful only if they stand for ideas, then either zero, none, and similar words are meaningless or else they stand for concepts.

It should not be thought, however, that Berkeley's failure to give an adequate empirical account of mathematical and logical terms necessarily signals a triumph for rationalism. In the first place, as we shall see in Chapter Seven, many twentieth-century empiricists have rejected the assumption that meaningful terms must always stand for ideas. In the second place, even if mathematical and logical terms did stand for concepts or innate ideas, rationalism would not thereby be proven true. It would obviously not follow from this alone that mathematical and logical terms—even less such terms as substance and God—express meaningful concepts with counterparts in external reality.

As was pointed out earlier, empiricism is not only a theory about the origin of our ideas, but also a theory about what is required in order to determine whether propositions concerning matters of fact are true or false. Empiricism in this second sense ordinarily rests, as does rationalism, upon a particular analysis of a priori knowledge. In the following discussion attention will be focused upon David Hume, the most thoroughgoing and probably the greatest of the classical empiricists.

Like Descartes, Hume distinguished between intuitive, or self-evident, a priori knowledge and demonstrative a priori knowledge. The former, it will be recalled, consists of propositions whose truth can be established immediately by rational insight; the latter, a set of propositions which can be deduced by logical or mathematical inference from intuitive propositions. This distinction was of great importance to Descartes, since his criteria of self-evidence (indubitability and clarity and distinctness) do not apply, at least directly, to demonstrative truths. An advanced theorem in Euclidean geometry, for instance, is not necessarily either indubitable or clear, although it may be both to somebody who has been able to grasp the long chain of inferences which constitute its proof. For Hume, this distinction is of less significance, since the particular criterion of self-evident truths which he selected serves equally well as a criterion of demonstrative truths. According to Hume the criterion for identifying a priori propositions, be they intuitive or demonstrative, is the unimaginability of their denials. (Hume sometimes used the term *inconceivability* instead of *unimaginability*. The latter term, however, is also used and is truer to his intent.) Consider, for instance, the self-evident proposition: "A square has four sides." The denial of this proposition is: "Squares do not have four sides." Since one cannot imagine a square without four sides, the original proposition must be a priori. Consider the demonstrative proposition: "The sum of the angles of a Euclidean triangle equals 180°." The denial of this proposition is: "The sum of the angles of a Euclidean triangle does not always equal 180°." But since any effort to imagine a Euclidean triangle with angles equaling more or less than 180° is doomed to failure, the demonstrative truth in question is also seen to be a priori by Hume's criterion.

Why Hume chose the unimaginability of its denial as a criterion for recognizing an a priori truth is not clear; nowhere in his work does he give a clear and decisive argument justifying this choice. Given this criterion, however, no knowledge of fact can be a priori. To confirm this, Hume says, one need only consider any randomly chosen proposition relating to a matter of fact. In every case it will be noted that the denial of that proposition is imaginable in a way that the denial of a mathematical or logical truth is not imaginable. Take, for instance, the proposition: "It will not snow next year in New York during the month of August." The evidence for this proposition is overwhelming; yet one can picture a snow storm in New York in August in a way that one cannot picture a square with only three sides. Consequently the proposition "It will not snow next year in New York during the month of August" cannot be a priori. The same is true of a proposition such as "An unsupported body in midair will fall to the ground." Since one can imagine an unsupported body flying upward rather than falling down to the ground, the proposition cannot be a priori.

From the fact that no matter of fact can be known a priori Hume concluded that no empirical or a posteriori proposition can be known with certainty. Knowledge of matters of fact is always and only probable, no matter how great the probability may be in a particular case. The central empiricist contention, however, has to do with the necessity of recourse to sense experience in order to validate knowledge of matters of fact, not with the merely probable nature of such knowledge. The argument for the latter comes first in the order of exposition only because the argument for the necessity of recourse to sense experience logically depends upon it. Freely worded, Hume's argument for the major empiricist claim is as follows:

(1) There are only two grounds of knowledge: reason and sense experience.
(2) Only knowledge acquired exclusively by reason is a priori.
(3) Only a priori knowledge is certain or necessary.
(4) No knowledge of matters of fact is certain or necessary.

∴ All knowledge of matters of fact depends upon sense experience.

One of the earliest and most important historical criticisms of this conclusion was presented by the late-eighteenth-century German philosopher Kant. Before proceeding to a discussion of Kant, however, it will be well to say something about Hume's justly famous analysis of causal knowledge. This analysis is an excellent illustration of the way in which empiricist principles are applied to concrete problems. Also, Kant claimed that it was this which woke him from his "dogmatic slumbers" and led to the formulation of his own position.

Hume's analysis of causality is in two parts. First he tries to show what the term cause properly means. He quickly disposes of the view that to say one event is the cause of another means that the first event has some power, force, or energy which enables it to bring the second into existence. In typical empiricist fashion Hume points out that there is not the slightest warrant for attributing to any event qualities or properties other than those we actually observe. He then argues that no event ever reveals to the senses any kind of force, energy, or power. We see, for instance, one moving billiard ball hit a second, and then we see the second billiard ball move in the direction determined by the point of impact of the first. But no matter how thoroughly we examine the first billiard ball we shall never discover in it any property or set of properties which by themselves could account for the movement of the second. If we were totally without experience of moving bodies, absolutely nothing would permit us to infer what would happen when the first ball hit the second. For all we could know, both would come to a dead stop, or the first would rebound in the direction from which it came, or the second would move upward in a straight line. The only thing that permits us to infer that the movement of the first ball would cause the kind of movement in the second ball that actually ensues is past experience with similar kinds of events.

What, then, do we mean when we say that one particular event is the cause of another? Hume gives two different answers to this question. One explanation is that these two events belong to classes of events which have been observed in the past and which we know from past experience to be regularly conjoined. The observable facts which give rise to the concept of causality and consequently the only ones in terms of which the concept may be defined are facts relating to the constant conjunction of similar types of events. Another answer to the question is that the thought of the first event leads us almost irresistibly to the thought of the second. If, for instance, we think of fire, we experience a kind of mental compulsion to think of smoke. This second definition is less fundamental than the first since the mental compulsion is a product of past experience. It was offered largely in order to explain why we so persistently tend to think of causality as a power existing in objects. It is Hume's contention that the compulsion by which the idea of the cause evokes the idea of the effect is erroneously construed as a power in the actual object rather than as a tendency of the mind to pass from one idea to another.

The second part of Hume's analysis aims to show that our reliance upon causal knowledge in predicting the future course of events is rationally unfounded. Hume does not say that men ought not to rely upon causal knowledge in planning for the future. For Hume, the question of *ought* or *ought not* does not even arise; we are psychologically compelled to act on this knowledge. If in our past experience we have observed that fire causes burns, we shall avoid fires instinctively. His point is rather that no rational argument can possibly justify our instinctive belief that events constantly conjoined in the past will be constantly conjoined in the future. That there can be no a priori justification of this belief follows from our being able to imagine future violations of any causal generalization. Of course, we do not really believe that contact with fire will in the future cause pleasurable rather than painful sensations; but we can imagine this, and what can be imagined cannot be impossible a priori. But neither can the belief be rationally supported by a posteriori arguments. All a posteriori arguments supporting a general principle like this must be based upon a posteriori principles of like or superior generality. If, for instance, one wishes to show by argument that all men are mortal, one could do so by pointing out that all men are animals and that all animals are mortal. But the term all animals denotes future animals as well as those existing in the past and present; and the only conceivable grounds for believing that future animals will be mortal is the fact that past animals have been mortal. Any plausible a posteriori proof of the principle that events conjoined in the past will continue to be conjoined in the future would therefore be circular—that is, it would have to be based on premises that can themselves be validated only by an appeal to the principle the proof was designed to establish.

KANTIANISM

Kant claimed to have instituted a revolution in philosophy as significant as Copernicus's revolution in astronomy. This claim is perhaps exaggerated; but his ideas have had an impact comparable to that of Descartes' and Hume's, and no one who hopes to understand or to help others understand modern philosophy dare pass Kant by.

At the beginning of Kant's career he was strongly attracted by rationalism, and throughout his life he remained convinced that reason was by itself competent to establish with complete certainty a large body of significant knowledge with respect to matters of fact. Like many other eighteenth-century thinkers Kant never wavered in his belief in the a priori truth of Newtonian mechanics, the crowning achievement of seventeenth-century science. Nor did he waver in the conviction that causal laws may be known a priori to have universal validity not only for the past and present but also for the future. Nonetheless, a close reading of Hume persuaded him that previous accounts of the nature of a priori knowledge had to be radically revised. His revisions are, in fact, so radical that it is misleading to call him a rationalist.

The most important difference between Kant and previous philosophers, whether rationalist or empiricist, lies in his point of departure. Whereas Descartes and Hume had each started from certain epistemological and metaphysical beliefs to go on to prove respectively the possibility and the impossibility of a priori knowledge of matters of fact, Kant started from what he took to be the fact that a priori knowledge of matters of fact exists and asked what metaphysical and epistemological theory could explain it. In other words, instead of asking *"Is* a priori knowledge of matters of fact possible?"* Kant asked *"How* is a priori knowledge of matters of fact possible?"

More precisely, Kant's question was: "How is synthetic a priori knowledge possible?" To understand this question it will be necessary to examine the terms *synthetic* and *analytic.* As Kant defines these terms, an analytic proposition is one whose predicate is contained in its subject in such a manner that anyone who clearly understands the meaning of the subject term will see intuitively that it contains the meaning of the predicate term. Consider, for instance, the proposition "All bodies are extended." The subject term is bodies; the predicate term, extended. But anyone who understands the full meaning of the term body will see that it includes the meaning of the term extended, for to be extended is to exist in space, and a part of the meaning of the term body is something existing in space.

A synthetic proposition, on the other hand, is one whose predicate is not contained in its subject, one whose subject term might be understood even by someone totally unaware of the meaning of the predicate term. One of Kant's examples is: "All bodies have weight." Weight is not a part of the meaning of the term body, as can be seen from the fact that a weightless object occupying space would still be called a body. The predicate of the proposition "All bodies have weight" is thus not contained in the subject. The proposition does not merely make explicit the meaning of "bodies": it asserts a fact about bodies.

Many of the empiricists, particularly Hume, regarded the distinction between analytic and synthetic propositions as merely another way of expressing the distinction between a priori and empirical knowledge. Our knowledge, said Hume, is either knowledge of "relationships between ideas," i.e., knowledge having to do with meanings of terms, or knowledge of "matters of fact," i.e., knowledge having to do with relationships between objects or properties actually existing in nature. The former is analytic and a priori; the latter is synthetic and a posteriori. There is not and cannot be any third kind of knowledge.

With this Humean and typically empiricist contention Kant disagrees. While granting that all a posteriori propositions are indeed synthetic and that all analytic propositions are a priori, he maintained that a third kind of proposition exists, viz., synthetic a priori propositions. These are propositions whose truth can be established by reason alone without recourse to sense experience but which do not merely make explicit the meanings of the terms involved. It is impossible to examine here all of the propositions which Kant claimed to be synthetic a priori. It will, however, be helpful to cite two examples and to indicate the empiricist rejoinder. Kant's most famous example is the mathematical proposition $7 + 5 = 12$. According to the empiricists, this proposition, when properly analyzed, turns out to be analytic a priori. The correct explication of the meaning of $7 + 5$ is:

$$1 + 1 + 1 + 1 + 1 + 1 + 1 + 1 + 1 + 1 + 1 + 1$$

Similarly, the correct explication of the meaning of 12 is:

$$1 + 1 + 1 + 1 + 1 + 1 + 1 + 1 + 1 + 1 + 1 + 1$$

Thus, anybody who clearly understands the meaning of $7 + 5$ will see that it includes, in this case by being identical with, the meaning of 12.

Another Kantian example of a synthetic a priori proposition is: "Causal laws that have held in the past will continue to hold in the future." Empiricists unanimously reject the claim that this proposition is an a priori truth. But in trying to prove Kant wrong, they encountered a problem. All propositions, they argue, are either analytic a priori or synthetic a posteriori. If, therefore, the proposition in question is not analytic a priori, the only apparent alternative is that it be synthetic a posteriori. However, most empiricists agree with Hume that experience is as incompetent as reason to pass on its truth or falsity; and if this is the case, the proposition does not conveniently fit into the class of synthetic a posteriori propositions, since most empiricists exclude propositions to whose truth or falsity experience cannot possibly testify from the class of a posteriori or empirical knowledge.

Hume himself did not seem to be fully aware of this problem, and it is not clear how he would have handled it. Some later empiricists, however, have met this challenge by arguing that the sentence "Causal laws that have held in the past will continue to hold in the future" does not express a proposition of any kind. It is not a knowledge claim at all, and it is therefore a mistake even to raise the question of its truth or falsity. Its grammatical form is the same as that of sentences which express genuine propositions, but its use in actual discourse is totally different. Its function is not to convey information about the universe, but rather to express a resolve to utilize causal knowledge acquired in the past as a guide to future behavior.

Rightly or wrongly, however, Kant starts from the assumption that synthetic a priori knowledge exists. What, then, is his answer to the question: "How is synthetic a priori knowledge possible?" His answer in brief is that synthetic a priori knowledge is possible only on the assumption that Locke was wrong in regarding the mind as an empty sheet of paper upon which experience alone writes. To know that a proposition about human experience is true universally, not only in the past and present but also in the future, it is necessary to assume that the mind legislates to rather than merely records experience. A crude analogy may help here. Suppose every member of the human race were born with normal eyesight and a pair of blue-tinted spectacles. Suppose further that these spectacles were so attached that it was impossible for anybody ever to remove them, even for a moment. Knowing this, could we not predict with certainty that every object presented to a human being would have a bluish tint? Would this not be a universal law of human experience? In fact, says Kant, something like this has taken place. The human mind has a certain structure, and whatever enters human experience will exhibit patterns imposed by that structure. It is only on this condition that synthetic a priori knowledge is possible.

The details of Kant's theory about the structure of the human mind will not detain us, although in passing it should be noted that Kant distinguishes between two different kinds of mental structures: (1) what he calls the *forms of human sensibility,* of which there are two, space and time; and (2) what he calls the *categories of human understanding,* of which there are twelve, including causality.

An important consequence of Kant's approach to the problem of knowledge is the distinction he is led to draw between *noumena,* or things as they are in themselves, and *phenomena,* or things as they appear to us in human experience. Of noumena, or things as they are in themselves independently of human observation, Kant maintains that no knowledge is possible except that they exist. It is only with respect to phenomena, or things as they enter into human experience under the forms of human sensibility and the categories of human understanding, that there can be knowledge. The attempt to understand noumenal realities leads inevitably to self-contradictions. It is here that Kant most radically breaks with traditional rationalist thinkers such as Descartes, Spinoza, and Leibniz; for by limiting a priori knowledge to the field of phenomena or aspects of reality shaped by human experience, Kant strikes at the heart of the rationalist tradition.

Chapter Four

THE SPECULATIVE

PHILOSOPHIES OF

PLATO AND ARISTOTLE

I N the last two chapters the discussion has centered on relatively specific philosophical problems. Although some of the solutions to these problems were highly speculative, we were not concerned with speculative philosophy as such. Our aim was rather to show how different philosophers came to grips with common problems. In the present chapter the focus shifts. Here our concern will be with speculative philosophical schemes themselves. Instead of discussing a variety of ways in which different philosophers attacked similar problems, we shall try to show how a single philosopher may attack a variety of problems with a few key concepts. Our choice of Plato and Aristotle for this purpose has been dictated by the fact that no other philosophers have had a greater historical impact.

PLATO

The names of Socrates and Plato are inextricably linked. Socrates himself wrote nothing, and he had little regard for books. One could not, he lamented, interrogate the written word. Some of this disregard for books carried over to his disciple Plato, who is reputed to have said that the most precious of his teachings could only be communicated orally. Nonetheless, Plato's complete extant work consists of almost thirty dialogues.

The principal interlocutor in all but a few of these dialogues is Socrates, and scholars have long been intrigued by the problem of determining to what extent the Socrates of these dialogues accurately represents the historical figure who was executed for worshipping false gods and corrupting the young. The consensus of scholars is that the dialogues in which Socrates is content to criticize popular belief and which end inconclusively best represent the historical Socrates. In those dialogues, on the other hand, where Socrates is more speculative and more confident in his assertions it is assumed that he is largely Plato's creation. Whether this scholarly surmise is accurate or not is a matter of relatively little importance. The important thing is the speculative philosophy itself, be it Socrates' or Plato's.

The cornerstone of Plato's speculative philosophy is his belief in the existence of a nonhuman and nonmaterial set of what he called *Ideas,* although to avoid confusion between Platonic Ideas and ideas conceived as events in human minds, many translators of the dialogues substitute the term *Forms.* Because these Ideas or Forms are not to be found either in the minds of human beings or in the material world presented to us by our physical senses, they are said to be *transcendent.* They lie beyond the ordinary world of human experience; their abode, so to speak, is in heaven. The chief properties of the Forms are eternality, immutability, and intelligibility, properties upon which Plato, in common with practically all classical and medieval philosophers as well as many modern philosophers, placed great value. Plato insisted that these properties cannot be found in material objects or in the immediate world of human experience. Physical objects come into existence and pass out of existence; while in existence they undergo a number of changes, and, according to Plato, they defy clear understanding. To mark the difference between the realm of eternal, immutable, and luminously intelligible Forms and the realm of temporal, changing, and essentially unintelligible bodies, Plato chose the terms Being and Becoming, respectively. Of Being, he speaks rapturously; of Becoming, disdainfully. Of Being there may be true knowledge through rational insight. Of Becoming there is only opinion derived from the unreliable physical senses.

To understand Plato one must obviously understand why he

believed in the Forms. His strongest argument is derived from mathematics, most especially from the science of geometry, which was only in the process of being discovered in his day but which made a powerful impression upon the intensely inquisitive Greek mind. The argument may be summarized as follows. Geometry consists of a body of eternal, immutable, and thoroughly intelligible truths. The objects of geometrical study cannot, however, be objects in the physical world, for no object in the physical world is eternal, immutable, or thoroughly intelligible. Therefore, for geometry to exist as a science, there must be a realm of nonphysical or transcendent objects to which it applies. (The gist of this argument emerges from a few examples. The geometer's straight line is a line without breadth, but where in the physical world does a line without breadth exist? The geometer's circle is perfectly round, every point of its circumference being at an exactly equal distance from its center. But where in physical nature does such a circle exist?) And once it is granted that there is a realm of knowable transcendent objects, what reason is there to limit this realm to the objects of geometry? May it not also be populated with the true objects of all other genuine knowledge?

Although this first argument is stronger than the second which will be stated shortly, Plato did not emphasize it. There is even reason to believe that Plato did not always regard the objects of mathematical study as pure Ideas or Forms. At times, he seemed to think of them rather as intermediary objects between pure Ideas and physical objects. An exploration of these refinements, however, would take us too far afield. For the purpose of initial orientation to Plato's thinking, the argument as stated will suffice.

Plato's second argument is based on the assumption that words have unique and unchanging meanings. This being the case, Plato argues, words cannot mean the multiple and changing objects of sense experience to which they are applied. Consider, for instance, the term beauty. No doubt, there are beautiful bodies in the world of Becoming, but none of these bodies is perfectly beautiful and all of them perish. There must, therefore, be an Idea or Form of beauty, and it is only by virtue of resembling or somehow participating in the Idea or Form of beauty that any physical object can properly be said to be beautiful. The true or ideal meaning of "beauty" lies beyond the realm of sense experience.

This argument is vulnerable on several counts. First, it is simply not true that words necessarily have unique and unchanging meanings. Many words are vague or ambiguous, and frequently the meanings of terms change considerably over a period of time.

Second, for a long time now logicians have recognized that words may have denotative and/or connotative meanings. A word is said to be *denotatively* meaningful if it applies to a class of objects, things, or events, and *connotatively* meaningful insofar as it designates a property or set of properties. For instance, the term bachelor is denotatively meaningful since it refers to a certain class of human beings; it is also connotatively meaningful insofar as it designates the properties of being male, human, adult, and unmarried. This crucial logical distinction between denotation and connotation was only obscurely discerned in Plato's day. It seems that Plato assumed falsely not only that words had unique and unchanging meanings, but also that meaning was restricted to denotation. Since the physical denotation of many terms does not exhaust their meaning and is in fact often the least important part of their meaning, he concluded that terms must have a nonphysical, or transcendent, denotation, viz., an Idea or Form.

Finally, this argument is closely related to and in great part depends upon a second. Since, Plato contended, any true proposition is eternally true, the fact expressed by the proposition must also be eternal. It was for this reason that Plato thought that finite beings in the world of Becoming could not be known. But why should the proposition "John Smith was born on May 23, 1943" not be eternally true even though the fact of John Smith's birth is a finite event in the world of becoming?

There are still other difficulties with Plato's theory of transcendent Forms. The most serious of these was posed in the dialogue *Parmenides,* named after a philosopher much older than Socrates whom Socrates is supposed to have met as a very young man. The dialogue is allegedly a report of that meeting. Parmenides points out that the theory of Ideas is irrelevant to human concerns. Human beings, says Parmenides, have to live in the world of Becoming, and the only useful knowledge is knowledge of the process of Becoming. If, therefore, the Forms are not related to the realm of Becoming in such a way that knowing them would help us to understand the temporal and mutable flow of events here below, we may as well forget about them.

But it is very difficult to see how the Forms could be related to the flux of temporal objects in the world of Becoming. Either the Forms participate in this flux of temporal objects or temporal objects are imperfect copies or resemblances of the Forms. Neither of these possibilities seems tenable. If the Forms participate in the multiple objects revealed to the senses, then they are not unique and indivisible entities nor are they transcendent. If, on the other hand, the Forms are archetypes of which objects in the world of Becoming are imperfect copies or resemblances, then Socrates must meet an objection that has become known as "the Third Man argument." Socrates seems to assume that if two men resemble one another, this is not because they possess similar or identical properties but rather because they both resemble the Form or Idea of Man. In other words, and more generally, Socrates supposes that in order for two objects to resemble one another, there must be an entity external to and different from each that mediates this resemblance. But, as Parmenides points out, if this is the nature of resemblance, then the resemblance between an object in the world of Becoming and its Idea or Form will require the existence of an entity external to and different from both. To establish the resemblance between the man Socrates and the Idea of Man, one must suppose the existence of a Third Man. Moreover, to establish a resemblance between the Third Man and Socrates or between the Third Man and the Idea of Man, it will be necessary to suppose the existence of still another entity, a Fourth Man, and so on *ad infinitum*. The dialogue ends with Socrates' reluctant admission that he cannot answer these objections.[1]

Another serious problem Plato faced was to explain how man can know the Forms. To say that man knows the Forms by the mind's eye or by direct rational insight, is in some sense an

---

[1] Some scholars regard this dialogue as evidence that Plato did not subscribe to the doctrine of Ideas. Others, pointing to the fact that the doctrine occurs in many dialogues and is essential to the understanding of many other Platonic views, regard it as a remarkable instance of self-criticism.

explanation, but by itself not a very satisfactory one. Man is a finite, mortal being whereas the Forms are infinite and eternal; and just as it has sometimes been asked how a finite being like man could possibly have an idea of an infinite being like God, many of Plato's contemporaries wondered how finite man could have knowledge of the infinite Forms. Plato's answer was to deny that man is merely finite and mortal. To be sure, man possesses a finite and mortal body, but this body is not a part of the nature or essence of man. Man, said Plato, is an immortal soul; he not only can but in fact has and will again live independently of the body.

Plato's theory about the relationship between soul and body is the most speculative part of his philosophy. There are four aspects to this theory: Plato believed in *personal immortality,* or the existence of the soul as a disembodied spirit after death; in *preexistence,* or the existence of the soul as a disembodied spirit prior to physical birth; in *reincarnation,* the doctrine that the soul inhabits at intervals a number of different bodies; and finally, in *transmigration,* the doctrine that the soul may be incarnated not only in human bodies but in the bodies of other animals. Plato's views on reincarnation and transmigration shall not concern us here. His views on preexistence and personal immortality, however, cannot be omitted from even the most cursory account of his philosophy.

According to Plato, the soul is completely released from the trammels of the physical world in the intervals between its incarnations. Having no attachment at all to the body, which Plato calls "the prison house of the soul," it lives in the realm of pure Being and has free access to the Forms or Ideas. When the time comes for the soul to be incarnated, it first passes through "the waters of forgetfulness," an immersion that considerably diminishes the soul's power of spiritual insight without wholly destroying it. Enough is left so that when the embodied soul encounters a physical copy of one of the Ideas, it senses a certain lack and is moved to remember more or less clearly the Idea itself. And here, he says, lies the true explanation of what man calls learning and teaching. To learn the true nature of any object is to recall its Ideal archetype or Form; to teach someone is simply to help him exercise this power of recall. Knowledge is really reminiscence; and genuine teaching is a matter of making explicit or bringing to consciousness what the student already knows.

To support this doctrine Plato cites in the *Symposium* the eternal discontent of the lover of beauty whose eye is turned wholly toward the beauties of the physical world. How can his insatiable longing be explained if one does not postulate the existence of a pure and perfect transcendent Idea of Beauty which haunts him? He also tries to show in the *Meno* how an ignorant slave boy, who has never been instructed in geometry, can be taught a fairly complicated theorem by the "Socratic method" of asking questions. If, Plato says, the boy learns the theorem without its actually being told to him, it is clear that in some sense he already knew it; and since he had not learned it in this life, he must have learned it in a state of preexistence.

Although these "proofs" of preexistence, if valid, create a presumption of immortality insofar as they establish that the soul can live independently of the body, they do not constitute, as Plato himself points out in the *Phaedo*, a conclusive proof of existence *after* physical death. To prove that the soul will survive the body, Plato argues in the following way. Death, he says, may be defined as the dissolution or breaking up of the parts of a complex whole. Therefore, since the soul is a simple being without parts, it cannot die. This proof of the immortality of the soul has a long history, having been used subsequently by, among others, Descartes. It has, however, come under heavy criticism. The counterargument is that although Plato's definition of death may serve passably well so far as physical bodies are concerned, it can hardly serve as a definition of the death of the soul, especially if it is granted that the soul is indivisible and without parts. If the soul is as different from physical bodies as Plato supposes, then a definition of death which applies to physical bodies could not apply to the soul and nothing may be rightly inferred from the fact that the soul cannot undergo physical death. One might as well argue that since the cessation of heartbeat is a feature of the death of mammals, a motor car cannot be destroyed since it has no heart.

ARISTOTLE

As a young student of Plato, Aristotle wrote dialogues similar in style and content to those of his master. The mature Aristotle, however, developed a doctrine distinctly his own, which has come down to us in the form of what were probably lecture notes. These notes betray no literary ambitions and treat subjects far more mundane than those treated in the Platonic dialogues. Plato came from an aristocratic Athenian family, which proudly traced its ancestry to one of the gods. Aristotle, by contrast, was the son of a provincial doctor, and in the end his sober respect for common sense prevailed over the love of noble ideas. This does not mean that Aristotle was so unphilosophical as to be incapable of following an argument wherever it led. And it should be remembered that the common sense of his day was not the common sense of today. In fact, many of his beliefs which may strike us today as quaint or even ridiculous were merely popular Greek ideas that escaped his critical scrutiny. Nonetheless, Aristotle's extant works display a curiosity about nature, a love of detail, and a matter of factness which are lacking in Plato's dialogues. If this substantial temperamental difference between the two men does not seem to be fully borne out by our account, it is because our concern is with Aristotle's more speculative doctrine, not with his very substantial contributions to logic, ethics, political theory, and natural philosophy, where his sobriety is most conspicuous.

Since Aristotle's independence as a philosopher began with his rejection of Plato's theory of transcendent Ideas, it is desirable to begin our discussion by asking why he rejected this theory. Aristotle answers this question succinctly in the first book of the *Metaphysics*. Echoing Parmenides, he says that the theory of Ideas simply fails to account for the world of Becoming. It is supremely important for us to know the world of sensible beings and the causes of the change and movement actually observed in that world. Static and unchanging Ideas which transcend this world obviously cannot help us achieve this goal. An understanding of the secrets of natural bodies and the principles which govern their development and interrelationships will not be gained by postulating the existence of an unobservable set of entities with all the properties of the natural bodies themselves except that they are immaterial and without motion. What is needed, according to Aristotle, is an accurate description of the pervasive and generic traits of natural processes and a set of genuinely explanatory principles. How well Aristotle succeeded in meeting this need is still often debated. No informed person will question, however, that the categories Aristotle employed, many of which were his own inventions, have profoundly influenced subsequent philosophical speculation and today are still deeply embedded in the popular mind. In the later Middle Ages his prestige was so great that he was frequently referred to as "The Philosopher."

In approaching the study of sensible bodies, Aristotle observes that questions of the form "What is x?" (where x stands for a sensible body) may elicit any one of four different kinds of answers. To take one of Aristotle's examples, a particular statue may be described as a block of marble, a likeness of a man, a work by a particular sculptor, or a monument to the memory of the man in whose likeness it is cast. The first answer has to do with the matter or stuff out of which the object is formed; the second, with the shape or form which the matter is given; the third, with the agent responsible for the object's existence; and the fourth, with the purpose or goal which the object serves. In Aristotle's terminology the four answers correspond respectively to the object's *material cause,* its *formal cause,* its *efficient cause,* and its *final cause.*

Although Aristotle's use of the term *cause* in the first and second senses has today disappeared from both common and philosophical parlance, the term is still used in the third and fourth senses. This is not surprising, for, as Aristotle was himself aware, the matter and the form of any sensible object are necessary and constituent parts of that object's nature in a way that its efficient and final causes are not. All sensible objects have both matter and form, and by virtue of being an amalgam of matter and form, an object becomes a recognizable entity with its own individuality and independent existence. The efficient and final causes, however, need not be known in order to identify a sensible object; they are better regarded as principles in terms of which we understand or explain its existence and/or form. To put the matter differently, the question "What is *x?*" should properly be answered simply by citing *x*'s matter and form. In pointing to an object's efficient or final causes, the question one is answering is "Why does *x* exist?" or "Why does it have such and such a form?"

In elaborating upon the concepts of matter and form Aristotle speaks of an object's *thisness* and *whatness.* Matter, he points out, is what individuates, what makes any particular object something that can be pointed to in order to distinguish it from another object with similar properties. However alike any two things may be, if they are really two distinct things they will occupy different locations in space and possess a matter entirely their own. But form is something that large numbers of objects may have in common; and if a particular "this" or lump of matter has been identified, perhaps by pointing, the question "What is it?" will be a request for a description of the object in terms of properties that it shares with other substances. Although the distinction between the matter and form or the thisness and whatness of any particular substance is of considerable theoretical importance, no independently existing sensible object will ever have one without the other. A sensible object is always a composite of matter and form. By a process of abstraction the mind may conceive one without the other, but pure matter and pure form do not exist in nature.

According to Aristotle, individual beings are subject to four kinds of motion. One of these is called *generation and destruction* —the kind of motion involved when an object comes into existence or passes out of existence. The other three types of motion are alteration, or *qualitative change,* as when a man's skin wrinkles or his hair turns white; increase or decrease in quantity, or *quantitative change,* as when a child becomes a man or an acorn becomes an oak; and change of place, or *locomotive change,* as when a planet revolves around the sun or a billiard ball moves across a billiard table. Each of these last three types of change involves a modification of an already existing object, and in this respect differs from generation and destruction. The most fundamental of the four types of change, however, is locomotion, or change of place. This is partly because locomotion is involved in all other kinds of change, but also because it can be found throughout the entire universe. The other three kinds of change are limited to the terrestrial, or what Aristotle called the *sublunar*, sphere of the universe.

This last point merits amplification. Aristotle's views with regard to the heavens are interesting in themselves and also important to an understanding of his entire conceptual scheme. According to Aristotle the heavens consist of fifty-five hollow spheres, one fitted inside the other. Each of these spheres revolves about the earth in a perfectly circular movement. The outermost sphere contains the fixed stars; in other spheres the sun, the moon, and the planets are embedded. These heavenly bodies differ from objects in terrestrial nature in three important respects. First, as already noted, their only change is locomotive change; nothing in this region of the universe comes into existence or passes out of existence, changes its qualities, or increases or decreases in size. Second, whereas the primary motion of sublunar bodies is rectilinear, the movement of heavenly bodies is always and only circular. Third, the matter out of which the heavens are composed is a highly rarefied element called ether, whereas the material elements of worldly bodies are fire, air, earth, and water.

To account for movement or change in the sublunar world Aristotle uses his notions of efficient and final causes. Consider Aristotle's favorite illustration of change in a natural body: the development of an acorn into an oak. The acorn obviously could not exist if there were no efficient cause of its existence, if there were no parent oak from which its existence could be derived. It is also evident that the acorn could never become an oak or undergo its specific form of development if it were not acted upon in the manner of an efficient cause by its natural environment. But, says Aristotle, the important thing about an acorn is that it may become an oak, and no attempt to explain this development exclusively in terms of efficient causes could possibly be successful. The *potentiality* of the acorn to be acted upon by its environment so as to become an oak lies within the acorn and cannot itself be attributed to the environment. After all, a sunflower seed exposed to the same environment would become a sunflower. Whence, then, comes the innate potentiality of the acorn? Since it cannot come from preexisting external causes, i.e., efficient causes, it can only come from its final cause or what Aristotle also calls its *entelechy*, or *actuality* or *completed form:* the as yet nonexisting physical oak which the acorn has the potentiality of becoming. In other words, to explain the acorn's becoming an oak, it is not enough to say that an acorn has been acted upon by external bodies. The acorn has within itself a principle of development determining the direction of its change. In the earlier stages of the acorn's growth that principle of development is a potentiality. In the final stages of its growth the potentiality is actualized, but the actuality or completed form is causally efficacious and therefore in some sense present from the very beginning of the whole process. What Aristotle wishes to emphasize is that in any natural process there are necessary and inevitable stages of development and that these stages of development are determined by the end product of the process itself. Of course, not every object realizes its potentialities; certainly, not all acorns become oaks. It may be that material conditions are unfavorable to the actualization of its potentialities. But if the object's potentialities are realized, this is because the substance's completed form is what it is and has played a genuinely causal role in the process of development.

As the example of the oak and the acorn illustrates, natural substances in the terrestrial world of earth, air, fire, and water may have indwelling final causes. However, natural substances also have final causes outside themselves. Aristotle tended to conceive the universe as a hierarchy of beings whose lower tiers exist for the sake of the higher. The indwelling entelechy of inorganic bodies is to rise if their matter is air or fire and to push toward the center of the earth if their matter is earth or water. But inorganic bodies are related to organic bodies as potentiality to actuality; their function is to serve the needs of organic life, and in addition to their indwelling entelechy they have a final cause in the organic life they support. Similarly, the lower forms of organic life such as vegetables and animals each have their own indwelling entelechies, but vegetables and animals also have a final cause outside themselves, which is to support man, the highest of organic beings. This hierarchy of causal dependence cannot, however, continue indefinitely. There must, Aristotle argued, be a first cause: something which exists in its own right, which contains within itself its own reason for being, which aspires to nothing it does not have, which is engaged in no process of development, and which consequently is pure actuality without any admixture of potentiality.

To this ultimate final cause Aristotle gave the name *God* or *Unmoved Mover*. He called it the Unmoved Mover because as pure actuality it cannot develop or change and because its existence is necessary to explain the entire cosmic process. He called it **God** because it is the highest and noblest of all beings; for what is higher than the ultimate object of all desire and all thought, and what but the ultimate object of desire and thought could move without itself being moved? However much impeded by the restraints of unfavorable material conditions, all things aspire toward God. Better yet, God draws everything to himself "even as the beloved moves the lover, unmoved itself."

Although in the *Metaphysics* Aristotle most often uses the terms God or Unmoved Mover in the singular, he also suggests that there may be more than one God or Unmoved Mover. In one passage he even suggests that there are fifty-five Unmoved Movers. The reason for this is as follows: According to Aristotle all sublunar motions are ultimately to be accounted for by reference to the movements of the heavenly spheres, and these in turn, by reference to the Unmoved Mover. Since the heavenly spheres are subject to no change except locomotion and since their motion is perfectly circular—a form of motion which Aristotle in common with most Greeks regarded as more perfect than rectilinear motion —they are obviously the link between the world of sublunar motion and God. But although the movement of each of the fifty-five spheres was perfectly circular and without a hint of imperfection when considered in itself, in order to explain the observed positions of the sun, the moon, and the planets Aristotle was obliged to assume that the inner spheres were out of step with the procession of the fixed stars, or the outermost sphere, and also out of step with one another. This called for an explanation, since if there is only one Unmoved Mover, one would expect that all of the spheres would move at a uniform speed. The explanation which comes most readily to mind is that each of the spheres is "in love with" a different Unmoved Mover and that ultimately the cosmic process requires for its explanation fifty-five separate principles of motion or ultimate final causes.

It is hardly necessary to labor the point that, having once rejected Plato's theory of transcendent Ideas, Aristotle was led to elaborate a very different picture of the cosmos. It will not, however, be amiss to point out that even at his most original Aristotle was still heavily in debt to Plato. This debt is most evident in two regards. First, although Aristotle denied the existence of pure Ideas or Forms and insisted that all natural objects are substances composed of form and matter, he maintained with Plato that forms alone are knowable. The thisness, or individuating matter of any particular object, cannot be known. In a sense, of course, it can be described. One can, for instance, say of an object that it is composed of water, earth, air, or fire. But to describe an object in terms of its material elements is not to identify that object in its individual concreteness. The result of all this is a paradox. On the one hand, Aristotle maintains that nature consists entirely of individuals. On the other hand, he declares that individuals as such cannot be known. What, then, is the object of knowledge? The obvious answer is the one Plato had already given: Forms.

Second, Aristotle is remarkably true to the spirit of Platonism when he exalts and glorifies mind. He does not construe man as a soul or mind forced for a time to dwell in the prison house of the body. On the contrary, he expressly declares that the soul is the form or function of the body in much the same way that cutting is the form or function of an axe and vision the form or function of the eye—from which it follows that the soul can have no existence separate from the body. Yet Aristotle could conceive of nothing higher or more noble than thinking for the sake of thinking. His God or Unmoved Mover engages in no activity other than thought; and his thinking, said Aristotle, is "a thinking on thinking," since it would be demeaning for God to turn his thought toward that which was material or merely potential. Moreover, Aristotle's ideal man is one who most completely imitates the divine by leading a largely contemplative life. In the order of living organisms, there are some, like plants, whose only activity is that of assimilating the matter of their environment; their soul is exclusively what Aristotle called *the nutritive soul.* Above the plants there are the lower animals, whose activity is not only nutritive but sensitive and appetitive as well. By virtue of their *sensitive souls* they may assimilate form without matter in the way that wax may take the form of a signet ring without absorbing its matter. At the same time the lower animals can experience pleasure or pain, and their *appetitive souls* consist of desires oriented toward securing pleasure and avoiding pain. Man alone, however, is capable of thinking; and the intellect or the *rational soul* of man is the agent of the highest activity that exists in sublunar nature. The rational soul does not exist to enhance the functioning of the lower activities. It is the other way around. The nutritive, the sensitive, and the appetitive souls exist for the sake of the rational soul. The highest of all human goods is speculation.

The fundamental concepts of the speculative philosophies of Plato and Aristotle do not have as widespread an appeal in the twentieth century as in the past. Plato's concept of a transcendent realm of Ideas strikes most of us as far-fetched. The best argument in its favor was that based on the apparent existence of non-material mathematical entities; but, as we shall see in Chapter Seven, twentieth-century philosophers have discovered a way of interpreting mathematical knowledge without positing the existence of such entities. And in the contemporary world Aristotle's crucial concept of final causality has for the most part either been abandoned altogether or modified beyond recognition. In psychology, where the term is still sometimes, though reluctantly, used, it usually means a special kind of efficient cause: namely, a causally efficacious human desire. A sculptor's desire to do homage to a public figure may, for instance, count as a cause of a statue's existence but not the prestige the statue later brings to its subject. The causally operative factor is the sculptor's desire, which antedated or accompanied the process of the statue's being made; the ends which the statue later served and which were not actually present during the process of creation are not causally relevant at all. Even in neo-Thomist philosophy, where the term final cause is retained and which in other respects is still heavily indebted to Aristotle, the concept has changed. The final cause of the acorn's becoming an oak is not the actual presence of the oak in the acorn but the will of God, who created the acorn with the intent that it become an oak. According to Aristotle God did not create the world, and he never gives it a thought.

Nonetheless, Plato and Aristotle cannot be dismissed. No one is really educated unless he is aware of the influential world outlooks that have prevailed in the history of his culture. If there were no other reason, it would be important to know them because they may have indirect, even insidious, effects upon our own thinking which only explicit knowledge can lay bare. But there is another and more compelling reason for studying the great speculative philosophers. As Kant said, and as every scientist knows, the world does not reveal its secrets easily. If we are to understand nature we must frame hypotheses and then seek within our limited experience reasons for accepting or rejecting them. But whereas almost any man of modest intellectual and imaginative powers can find reasons for accepting or rejecting a hypothetical world view, devising one that will survive for centuries is the work of genius. A speculative philosophical scheme such as Plato's or Aristotle's thus exhibits both the glory and the frailty of the human mind. It is at the same time a reminder of human ingenuity and a lesson in humility.

░░

Chapter Five

PROBLEMS

IN THE PHILOSOPHY

OF RELIGION

.

I N this chapter the word religion will be used to refer exclusively to those systems of belief, such as Judaism, Christianity, and Islam, which include the concept of a single, transcendent, omnipotent, and benevolent being who created the physical world out of nothing. This use of the term does not fully accord with accepted usage. Many of the world's religions are polytheistic, and some Buddhists do not believe in God at all. Furthermore, in many monotheistic religious systems the concept of God is different from the one stated. Plato, for instance, conceived of God as a being who shaped preexisting matter so as to make it conform to the Ideas or Forms. For Spinoza God and Nature were one; in his system God was immanent, not transcendent. Since, however, a single chapter cannot cover all of the world's religions and since the Judaeo-Christian tradition is most familiar to those reared in the Western world, the definition proposed is the most service-able. In view of the centrality of the concept of God, we shall begin our discussion with an examination of the major arguments used to prove his existence.

SOME ARGUMENTS FOR THE EXISTENCE OF GOD

The Ontological Argument. The only major argument for the existence of God which has the distinction of being completely a priori is the ontological proof. Its first formulation was by the eleventh-century philosopher St. Anselm; in slightly modified form it was also used by Descartes, Spinoza, and Leibniz. Its principal antagonists were St. Thomas, Hume, and Kant. Anselm argued in the following way. God, he said, is "a being than which no more perfect can be conceived." And since it is more perfect to exist than not to exist, God would not be the most perfect being that can be conceived unless he existed. Therefore, God exists. The essence of the argument seems to be that the concept of a nonexistent God is logically impossible or self-contradictory. From the logical impossibility of the concept of a round square one must infer the falsity of "A round square exists." In like manner, from the logical impossibility of the concept of a nonexisting God one must infer the falsity of "God does not exist." And if "God does not exist" is false, then its contradictory "God does exist" must be true.

In his own day Anselm's argument was criticized on the grounds that perfection does not imply existence; if it did, then utopia or a perfect society would exist. Anselm pointed out in rebuttal that there is a difference between the concept of a being such as God who possesses *all* perfections and the concept of utopia to which we attribute only a limited number of perfections of a special kind. Moreover, it seemed evident to Anselm and others that no created being could possibly possess all perfections, for if it did, it would not be a created being but rather a second god, which is absurd. To take account of this point, it is perhaps best to reformulate the argument in the following way:

(1) God is a being who possesses all perfections.
(2) Existence is a perfection.

∴ God exists.

A later criticism comes from Hume. He argued against Anselm's proof on the grounds that the nonexistence of God could be imagined and that it is impossible to construct an a priori proof for any proposition whose contradictory can be imagined. This counterargument of Hume's will probably appeal to those who accept Hume's criterion for identifying a priori propositions. It should be remembered, however, that Hume's criterion is itself debatable. Furthermore, Hume missed the point of Anselm's argument; Anselm was trying to show, among other things, that anyone who clearly and properly conceived of God could not possibly imagine him not to exist—that the nonexistence of God is as unimaginable as a round square.

Still later, Kant attempted to break down the ontological argument. Anselm's claim, translated into Kant's terminology, was that the proposition "God exists" is a synthetic, a priori proposition. But if Kant's metaphysics and epistemology are correct, there can be no synthetic, a priori knowledge of any matter of fact transcending the phenomenal world; and, of course, Anselm's God is transcendent.

To this argument Kant added a second—one which does not require for its validity an acceptance of Kant's own philosophical system. According to this argument, propositions asserting that something exists are of a totally different kind from those asserting that a given subject has a certain property. Consequently, any argument, such as Anselm's, which attempts to derive a conclusion of the first kind from premises of the second kind must be invalid. Consider the two propositions: (1) Bachelors are unmarried men, and (2) Bachelors are irascible. The first of these is analytic: its predicate "unmarried men" is contained in its subject "bachelor." The second is synthetic: its predicate "irascible" adds to the concept of bachelor. In both cases, however, a property is genuinely predicated of the proposition's subject. Consider now by way of contrast: (3) Bachelors exist. Grammatically, "exist" is a predicate, but logically it is not. The reason is that existence is not a property which may be predicated of anything. One may affirm that bachelors exist, but in making that affirmation one is neither making explicit the meaning of nor adding to the concept of bachelor. The concept of a bachelor remains the same whether one thinks of bachelors as existing or as not existing. In brief, then, Anselm's argument fails because it *falsely* assumes that the grammatical predicate "exists" is also a logical predicate and that consequently the premises of his arguments ("God is a being who possesses all perfections" and "Existence is a perfection") are of the same kind as his conclusion ("God exists").

Kant's contention that existence is not a proper logical predicate and that existential statements are of a radically different kind from others has met with wide favor in the twentieth century. Even if one waives this difficulty, however, and grants that existence is a genuine logical predicate, Anselm's argument is still unacceptable to most empiricists. Consider the conclusion of the argument: "God exists." If this proposition is meaningful it must be either analytic or synthetic. If it is analytic, all that it states is that the concept of God implies the concept of existence, that it would be improper to use the word God to refer to a being who did not exist, or (as St. Thomas put it) that if we think of God we must think of him as existing. But from the fact that the word God would be improperly applied to a being who did not exist or that the concept of God involves the concept of existence, one cannot properly infer that God actually exists. If, on the other hand, the proposition "God exists" is synthetic—that is, if the concept of God does not analytically entail the concept of existence, and if the proposition asserting his existence is similar to the proposition "Bachelors are irascible"—then in order to establish that God has the property of existence one would first have to have experience of God. Since, however, God transcends human experience, this is impossible.

The Cosmological Argument. The cosmological argument, like the other arguments still to be discussed in this chapter, is ordinarily regarded as a posteriori. Its first premise is that every object in nature is causally dependent in some sense of the word cause upon at least one other object. It follows that either (a) the objects in nature constitute an infinite chain or hierarchy of beings, or (b) there exists outside nature a first cause upon which the totality of natural beings depends. But, the argument continues, since an infinite regress in the order of nature is logically impossible, the cosmos must have an external cause, and this external cause is what we mean by "God." Aristotle's argument for the existence of an Unmoved Mover is the oldest version of the cosmological argument known to us; and although in the Christian era the argument has been given still other versions, the logical pattern is similar in every case.

One counterargument is that the being whose existence this argument purports to establish is not religiously significant. A first cause or an Unmoved Mover is not a being to whom we owe worship. As William James put it, a first cause is a "metaphysical monster." It is not the God of the Old Testament prophets, nor the God who was incarnated in human form and died on the cross. Even theoretically the concept of a first cause is unsatisfying, for, if the first cause is genuinely transcendent, then like Kant's noumenal world we can know nothing about it except that it exists. And we obviously cannot take that of whose nature we are totally ignorant as a principle of explanation for everything else.

A second counterargument calls into question the impossibility of an infinite regress. Those who hold that an infinite regress in the order of natural beings is impossible claim that this is a self-evident proposition; but in view of the difficult problems associated with the notion of self-evidence, this claim ought to be treated with caution. Moreover, it is difficult to see why the person who asserts that every natural being must have a cause is led to suspend the search for further causes after having postulated the existence of a supernatural being. It may be that a self-evident principle universally applicable to natural beings is not applicable to a supernatural being. But ought this to be assumed without reason? And what reason can be given?

The Teleological Argument. The teleological argument is also known as "the argument from design." Like the cosmological argument it has many different versions with a common underlying logical pattern. The skeleton of the argument is as follows: Nature as a whole has a number of properties analogous to the properties of human artifacts; and since human artifacts are known to be designed by intelligence, it is reasonable to infer that Nature is also designed by intelligence. In the eighteenth century, when large numbers of people believed that Newtonian physics had finally unlocked the secrets of the universe, the argument often took the following form: Nature is like a giant clock. When we see an ordinary clock we declare that there must be a clockmaker; so too when we regard the spectacle of Nature, we must by parity of reasoning acknowledge a maker of Nature.

This argument, if logically sound, goes farther than the cosmological argument toward establishing the existence of a deity with the properties traditionally attributed to the Jewish or Christian God. The cosmological argument, as we know from its Aristotelian version, is compatible with a concept of the first cause as without will or purpose. And although those who have employed the cosmological argument did in fact believe that the first cause was an intelligent being, there is nothing in the argument itself to support this conclusion. The teleological argument, on the other hand, does tend to establish the existence of a purposeful being endowed with intelligence, since men create clocks to serve their goals and employ intelligence in the process. But there is nothing in the teleological argument to suggest that the designer of the universe is either omnipotent or benevolent; nor is there anything in the argument which could be used to establish that the designer of the universe created it out of nothing. The argument is perfectly consistent with a conception of a creator who designed the world for evil purposes and with the Platonic conception of God as a being who modeled the world out of pre-existing matter that in many respects successfully resisted his efforts. Thus, even if the argument is logically impeccable, its religious significance is limited.

Is it, however, logically impeccable? Since the argument rests upon an analogy between human artifacts and Nature or the Cosmos as a whole, it cannot be logically stronger than the analogy. How good, then, is the analogy? In what respect is Nature said to be like human artifacts and how strong is the resemblance? According to the argument the point of resemblance is orderliness and the degree of resemblance nearly perfect. Just as a clock is a unified structure each of whose parts is intricately adapted to the others, so Nature is a unitary system of natural bodies governed by universal laws that regulate their movements.

One difficulty here is that the case for monism (the technical term for the conception of Nature as a single, unified whole) rests more heavily upon dubious metaphysical assumptions and pious hopes than upon known facts. Nobody, of course, denies that there are regularities and patterns of order in Nature; and nobody, of course, can be sure that these observed regularities are not like pieces of a jigsaw puzzle. In time other pieces may be discovered, and when enough pieces have been accumulated they may fit together to give us a single overall picture. But an argument must be based upon the evidence presently available, not upon the evidence we hope to have in the future. And the evidence presently available is as favorable to the hypothesis of a pluralistic universe as to that of a monistic universe. In fact, it is often said that the teleological argument for the existence of God is circular, since the usual grounds for belief in Nature as a unitary system is a belief in Nature as the product of a single divine intelligence.

There is another logical difficulty with the teleological argument. The argument states that Nature is like human artifacts in exhibiting order and that since human artifacts are known to be products of intelligence, it must be inferred that Nature is a product of intelligence. But if it could be shown that there are systems of order in nature which are not observably due to intelligence, the argument will lose much of its plausibility. And what is more evident than that many such systems exist? Individual living organisms, ant heaps, and colonies of bees exhibit patterns of order no less marked or obvious than the products of human invention, but unless one assumes the existence of a deity (which is precisely what the argument is intended to prove) there is no compelling reason to believe that these nonhuman patterns of order have an intelligent cause.

The Argument from Miracles. The expression "argument from miracles," though standard, is somewhat misleading. It suggests that there exists a class of events called miracles which can be *defined* without reference to divine agency and that one argues from the existence of these events to the existence of a deity as their cause. In fact, however, the clearest and simplest definition of a miracle is an event caused directly by divine agency; and when miracles are so defined the substantive question is not whether miracles require explanation in terms of a deity but rather whether miracles actually occur.

Alleged miracles fall into two classes. The first class consists of events which are said to contradict well-established laws of nature. The second class consists of events which, though they do not actually contradict well-established laws of nature, are said to be inexplicable in terms of natural law. The two classes of miracles are not always easy to distinguish, largely because of vagueness in the term laws of nature. The distinction can, however, be illustrated by examples. Christ's walking on water is a fairly clear-cut instance of a violation of a law of nature, namely the law of gravity. Many authenticated cures at Lourdes and other religious shrines are examples of events for which there appear to be no natural explanation, although it is difficult to name a reasonably well-defined law of nature that they contradict.

With respect to any alleged miracle two questions may be asked: (1) Have we rational grounds for believing that the event actually took place as described? (2) Assuming that it did take place, must we explain the event as the result of divine agency? To establish the existence of a genuine miracle it is obviously necessary to give good reasons for answering *both* questions in the affirmative, but to refute the claim that a miracle has taken place it is enough to give good reasons for a negative answer to *either* of the two questions.

The classic argument against alleged miracles that violate the laws of nature was stated by Hume. In brief, his argument was that an established law of nature is by definition one for which there is such an overwhelming mass of evidence that evidence for its violation could never be anywhere near so strong. As Hume pointed out, most alleged miracles took place in the past, and present-day belief rests wholly on human testimony. But, he said, in view of the mass of evidence in support of natural laws and the many well-documented cases of human deceit and self-deception, it is always more rational to put our trust in the law of nature than in the human testimony offered on behalf of the alleged miracle. In fact, he considered the evidence for the laws of nature so strong that it would be irrational to believe in their violation even if one personally witnessed an alleged miracle. Suppose, for instance, that you personally saw a man who claimed to be Christ walk across the pond in Central Park. If you are rational, will you not believe that you witnessed a trick or that your eyes deceived you rather than that the man is Christ reincarnated?

Since Hume defined a miracle as a violation of the laws of nature, he did not even consider the second class of alleged miracles: those for which there is no natural explanation in terms of existing knowledge of nature but which do not, so far as we know, violate any law of nature. In many cases alleged miracles falling into this class may be questioned on the grounds that it is irrational to believe the facts as reported; but there are many others that have been so thoroughly authenticated as to be beyond reasonable dispute. In these latter cases the question is thus whether it is more reasonable to attribute the facts to the operation of laws of nature as yet unknown or to God. It seems that a fully conclusive argument either way is out of the question. Any observed fact which does not clearly violate a known law of nature might conceivably be explicable by some unknown natural law. On the other hand, so long as a fact has not been explained naturalistically, it would be irrational to reject a nonnaturalistic explanation out of hand.

There is, however, a serious question as to whether anyone would be tempted to explain a fact for which no natural explanation is presently available as an act of God unless he already believed in God's existence. To put the same point somewhat differently, there is reason to believe that any argument for the existence of God based upon alleged miracles would be circular. The class of events for which there is no presently available natural explanation is very large, and only a relatively small number of events in this class are alleged to be miracles. As a rule, those selected are events which could plausibly be construed as rewards for piety or punishments for sin. But if one did not antecedently believe in a just and merciful God, how can one explain this principle of selectivity? The fact that there are some events for which we lack a natural explanation but which could be construed as rewards for piety or punishments for sin does not by itself constitute adequate evidence for the existence of God. A sound argument would require that the percentage of as yet unexplained natural events having this character be higher than one would expect on the assumption that they are all explicable in terms of unknown natural causes. Otherwise, we would have to conclude that God is no more just and merciful than Nature itself.

In conclusion it should be noted that the "argument from miracles" suffers from a failing noted with respect to the cosmological and teleological arguments. At most it establishes the existence of a nonnatural being who sometimes intervenes in the course of natural affairs. It does not prove the existence of an omnipotent and fully benevolent being who created the world.

THE PROBLEM OF EVIL

The most popular as well as the most telling argument against the existence of God has its point of departure in the fact of evil. It should first be noted, however, that there are three species of evil. One has traditionally been called *physical evil,* by which is meant physical disability and suffering; another is *moral evil,* or sin and imperfection of character. The third form of evil has no name sanctioned by tradition, and, with the exception of Descartes, philosophers have, somewhat surprisingly in view of their professional bias, tended to give it little attention. Here it will be called *intellectual evil,* by which is meant ignorance and false belief.

The argument against the existence of God based on the fact of evil is as follows. If God is both benevolent and omnipotent, then he would not permit the existence of evil; since, however, evil does exist, a benevolent and omnipotent deity cannot exist. In another but equivalent version, the argument is that if evil exists, this is either because God *cannot* prevent it, in which case God is not omnipotent, or because God *will not* prevent it, in which case he is not benevolent; but a being which is either not omnipotent or not benevolent cannot be God, since omnipotence and benevolence are both defining properties of a divine being.

To see the common logical pattern of these arguments, consider the following three statements:

(1) God is omnipotent.
(2) God is benevolent.
(3) There is evil.

The third statement, it is said, is indisputably true, but the truth of this third statement is incompatible with the joint truth of (1) and (2).

To meet the challenge posed by this argument the theist must show either that evil does not exist or else that the divine attributes of omnipotence and benevolence may be properly interpreted in such a way as to make the truth of all three statements logically possible. In general, theistic solutions to the problem of evil have been of the latter kind, but it will be convenient to begin the discussion by considering a famous argument designed to establish the non-existence of evil.

This argument has been most forcefully stated by St. Augustine, the first of the great Christian philosophers. He maintained that evil has no positive existence; it is merely an absence or privation of good. Physical evil is an absence of physical well-being, moral evil, an absence of moral perfection, and intellectual evil, an absence of omniscience. In support of this conception of evil, Augustine draws an analogy between good and light, on the one hand, and evil and darkness, on the other. Just as light is the positive reality of which darkness is merely a privation, so good is the positive reality of which evil is merely a privation.

The logical merit of this argument is difficult to assess without a precise definition of the key terms, absence and privation. Unfortunately, the analysis of these terms is exceedingly difficult and controversial. Those who find the argument unconvincing, however, tend to argue that Augustine has confounded a distinction of value with a distinction of ontological status. Light and good are positive realities in the sense that they are humanly valuable, whereas darkness and evil are disvalues or negative quantities in the sense that they impede human well-being. But in existential status, as facts in nature, dark and evil are both positive realities. Apart from considerations of human value or disvalue, the conception of darkness and evil as the absence of light and good is in no way superior to a conception of light and good as the absence of dark and evil.

Theistic philosophers who accept the reality of evil and attempt to reconcile it with God's omnipotence and benevolence have tended to offer some version of two main arguments. The first is based on the contention that the term benevolence when applied to God has a different meaning than when applied to men. A fully benevolent earthly parent would, of course, do everything within his power to make his children healthy: physically, spiritually, and intellectually. But God is not a finite parent of a limited number of children. God is the Father of all creation. His goodness, therefore, expresses itself in efforts to assure a maximum of perfection in creation as a whole, not just the maximum good for human beings. Although this view has been held by a large number of theistic philosophers, it was perhaps most clearly stated by Leibniz, who chose the term *metaphysical good* to refer to the proper object of God's benevolence. For Leibniz, as for many others, a metaphysically good world is one possessing a maximum variety of beings. He argued that in order to assure this maximum variety of beings, God was obliged to create a number of imperfect creatures subject to evil. Without them creation would lack the fullness of perfection. Dissonant chords in a musical composition, though ugly in themselves, are, Leibniz pointed out, often necessary to the beauty of the whole.

The chief objection to this argument is that when God's benevolence is interpreted as a concern for metaphysical perfection at the expense of human well-being God ceases to be a worthy object of worship. A world with a great variety of beings subject to evil can be plausibly construed as more satisfying aesthetically than a less variegated world without evil. No doubt, many men vastly prefer a Shakespearean tragedy to a light comedy. But it is one thing to stage a play with the intent of moving the spectators by depicting evil, another thing altogether, to be responsible for the real suffering of living human beings. Moreover, if we take the aesthetic analogy seriously and assume that metaphysical perfection is a good because of the gratification it affords the spectator, we may be forced to conclude that God created the world for his own pleasure. Neither the man suffering from a terminal cancer nor the human witnesses of his suffering are likely to derive much satisfaction from the thought that his pain is a necessary incident in a perfect divine scheme. The aesthetic distance and overall perspective on the human drama required to appreciate this scene appear to be possible only for God.

The second argument begins with an analysis of the term omnipotence. For one group of philosophers known as *voluntarists* God's will is completely unfettered. Although God obviously did not create round squares there is nothing in his nature which would have made this impossible. According to a second school known as *intellectualists,* God's will is subordinate to his intellect, and given the nature of his intellect, he could not create the logically impossible. If the voluntarist thinks that inability to do the logically impossible is a limitation on God's omnipotence, he simply misunderstands the nature of omnipotence. To be omnipotent is to be able to do what one wills without outside hindrance; since God's intellect is a part of his nature, self-determination by his own intellect could not possibly be a limitation of his power. It follows that God's omnipotence does not imply the ability to create any kind of world at all; the only kind of world he can create is a logically possible world. It also follows that if the best of all logically possible worlds necessarily contains some evil, the existence of evil is not logically incompatible with the existence of an omnipotent and benevolent deity.

But does the best of all logically possible worlds necessarily contain evil? Affirmative answers to this question usually take the following form. If God had endowed men with an infallible instinct for truth, beauty, and goodness he would have had to deny man freedom of the will, or the ability to choose for himself, with all that this entails. And since freedom of the will is the highest of all human goods, a world without evil but also without freedom of the will would be inferior to a world with both evil and freedom of the will. In sum, the world we live in is, in Leibniz's phrase, "the best of all possible worlds" despite the evil it contains; these evils are a necessary and inevitable consequence of man's misuse of his free will and are more than compensated for by the value of free will itself.

Three questions arise with respect to this argument. First, does all the evil in the world result from a misuse of free will? It would not be implausible to lay the blame for Dachau and Hiroshima upon a misuse of free will. But what about natural catastrophes such as earthquakes and floods? It might be said that the enormity of man's abuse of free will is not sufficiently punished by the evils to which it directly leads and that God is obliged by his sense of justice to supplement evils such as Dachau and Hiroshima with natural catastrophes to make the account come out right. If so, even natural catastrophes would be indirectly caused by an abuse of free will. But since natural catastrophes strike the innocent and the good as well as the evil, this explanation seems to commit us to the questionable moral doctrine of inherited sin.

Second, the argument presupposes that freedom consists of the ability to choose evil as well as good and that human freedom is therefore diminished to the extent that God disposes man to choose good rather than evil. These presuppositions are questionable. Is a man of good moral character who cannot even conceive doing a base or ignoble act less free than a man of bad character? Is a parent who exerts himself to the utmost to develop good moral character in his children thereby diminishing their freedom?

Third, even if we accept these presuppositions and define freedom as the ability to choose between good and evil, is freedom so supreme a value as to compensate for the evils to which it leads? Does the value of Hitler's having been able to choose the death of millions of Jews outweigh the sufferings he imposed upon his victims?

FAITH, REASON, AND REVELATION

Faith is a term with strong honorific associations, and in the Christian tradition it ranks with hope and love among the highest of virtues. It is, however, difficult to state precisely what is understood by faith, and in order to present a clear appraisal of it, several ambiguities in the term will have to be examined. A person who believes that the evidence he possesses for a given proposition is conclusive obviously does not have faith in that proposition. One *knows*, for instance, that two plus two equals four; one does not believe this on faith. Faith occurs only with regard to propositions for which the evidence is less than conclusive. But here three cases must be distinguished: (1) the case in which available evidence, though less than conclusive, indicates that the proposition is true, (2) the case in which available evidence indicates that the proposition is false, and (3) the case in which the evidence available neither supports nor negates the proposition.

In regard to the first case, faith is ordinarily construed as an attempt to buoy up our confidence in the proposition so as to make it possible for us to act appropriately. To take a nonreligious example, imagine a man who has good reason to believe in a friend's loyalty but for some reason finds himself assailed by doubts that make it difficult for him to accord his friend the degree of trust that is rationally warranted. Here faith would consist in an attempt to banish unreasonable doubts by fixing firmly in mind the evidence telling in his friend's favor. In like fashion, a man might believe that the existence of God is rationally warranted. Since, however, the rational warrant is less than conclusive, there is room for gnawing doubts, and he may find himself straying from the religious way of life. Here faith would again consist in an attempt to reinforce his belief by a periodical reexamination of the evidence. It is unlikely that anybody would criticize faith so construed as either irrational or immoral. On the contrary, faith of this kind is positively demanded by reason itself and is in every way highly commendable. If this were the whole of what is meant by faith, there would be no philosophical problem of faith.

As a matter of historical fact religious faith has not always been construed in this way. Some Christian thinkers, most notably Søren Kierkegaard, the nineteenth-century Danish philosopher who is widely regarded as the father of existentialism, have gone so far as to maintain that many religious beliefs are logically absurd or self-contradictory. Kierkegaard said that this was true of the Christian doctrines of the trinity and of the dual nature of Christ. Reason, he says, flatly affirms that there can be no reality corresponding to the self-contradictory notions of God as three separate persons but one substance, or of Christ as wholly divine and wholly human at one and the same time. If, therefore, there is such a thing as Christian faith, it will necessarily be in open defiance of reason.

When faith is understood in this way, one is led to ask whether we are capable of it. If anyone is convinced that the doctrines of the trinity and the dual nature of Christ are self-contradictory, then he could reasonably be expected to have as much difficulty believing them as he would have believing in the existence of round squares. Kierkegaard was very much aware of this difficulty, and he sometimes characterized his philosophical endeavor as an attempt to answer the question: How can I become a Christian? In some passages he answered that if he tried hard enough God might by an act of grace grant him the power to believe in defiance of reason. Kierkegaard did not, however, seem to be fully satisfied with this answer; for in other passages he abandons the idea of faith as a species of belief altogether and interprets it rather as an attitude of intense concern for one's own personal fate. The savage who worships an idol with passion has faith, he said, whereas the Christian who worships the true God without passion does not.

Unlike Kierkegaard, most religious thinkers have insisted that no true dogma ever contradicts reason Few, however have maintained that all their religious beliefs can be supported rationally by conclusive or even by probable arguments. St. Thomas who allowed a greater place to reason than have many Christian philosophers, granted that a number of dogmas must be accepted by faith or revelation alone. The dogmas of the trinity, of the dual nature of Christ, and of creation out of nothing do not, according to St. Thomas, contradict reason. So far as reason is concerned, they may be true. But whether they are in fact true or in fact false is something which reason has no competence to decide.

In regard to this third case several questions arise. First, a large number of philosophers, especially in the twentieth century, maintain that we can always, at least in principle, determine the truth or falsity of any genuine proposition. In fact, according to one widely held theory of meaning called the "verification theory" (which will be discussed in Chapter Seven) a proposition whose truth or falsity could not conceivably be decided by reason would be meaningless. These thinkers grant that given the present state of human knowledge there are a number of genuine propositions whose truth or falsity cannot be presently established, but the difficulties are purely practical and may well be overcome in the future. Consequently, they argue that the only rational attitude to adopt in such cases is the suspension of both belief and disbelief. If, for instance, the proposition "God exists" is a genuine proposition and if evidence presently available indicates neither its truth nor falsity, reason demands that we adopt the attitude of an agnostic until more evidence turns up. If we chose to believe in the absence of rational evidence, we would block the road to further inquiry.

Second, some persons argue against the possibility of faith of this kind in much the same way that one argues against the possibility of faith as conceived by Kierkegaard. To believe, they say, is to give intellectual assent to a proposition; but just as one cannot give intellectual assent to a proposition that one knows to be self-contradictory, so one cannot give intellectual assent to a proposition for which one has no evidence. It is doubtful, however, whether the term belief should be understood in this way. Most philosophers tend to agree with Hume, who characterized belief as a feeling or sentiment often but not always or necessarily associated with the operations of the intellect. Nonetheless, this particular criticism of faith does have the merit of underscoring a point made long ago by Socrates: when a belief is not supported by evidence, it is often difficult to sustain. In Socrates' words, it is not tied down and tends "to run away from us." The truth of this observation has been eloquently confirmed by religious literature discussing "the trials of faith."

Third, if one waives the first and second difficulties, assuming both the meaningfulness of religious propositions despite the incompetence of reason to establish their truth or falsity and the possibility of sustaining belief in propositions for which rational evidence is lacking, why should belief in such propositions be considered an act of moral virtue? The usual answer to this question is that faith is a condition of individual or social well-being. Space prohibits even a cursory review of the many different concrete forms this answer has taken. One illustration from the seventeenth-century French philosopher Blaise Pascal will have to suffice. The argument is known as "Pascal's wager." Either, said Pascal, Christianity is true, or it is false. If it is true, then by believing one can hope to gain an eternal life of heavenly bliss whereas by disbelieving one can expect an eternal life of torment in hell. If, on the other hand, Christianity is false, then by believing one risks the loss of a few earthly pleasures which disbelief would permit one to enjoy. Since, however, Christianity may be true and since it is irrational to forego the chance of heavenly bliss or to risk eternal torment for the sake of a few paltry worldly pleasures, the rational man will be a believer.

In addition to faith and reason, an often cited ground of religious belief is revelation or authority, be it of religious scriptures or of an ecclesiastical authority. It is, however, difficult to see how revelation or authority could be properly regarded as a wholly independent source of religious belief. If one takes the Bible to be an authoritative revelation of divine will, this means that one subscribes to the proposition "The Bible expresses the will of God." And though one could subscribe to this proposition by virtue of belief in a second authority, it is obvious that the appeal to authority cannot go on indefinitely. At some point one must either try to establish one's right to belief in the authority one accepts on rational grounds or recognize that it rests upon nonrational faith. If it rests upon nonrational faith, the philosophical problems will be of the kind with which we are already familiar.

The most common arguments in support of any given religious authority, all of which were used by St. Thomas in support of the Bible as divine revelation, are: (1) The revelation was accompanied by miracles, (2) the revelation includes prophecies which have come true, and (3) the revelation has elicited the belief of large numbers of persons who bore testimony to its truth by their willingness to suffer and even to die on its behalf.

Chapter Six

丛丛丛丛丛丛丛丛丛丛丛丛丛丛丛丛丛丛丛丛丛丛丛丛丛丛丛丛丛丛丛丛丛丛丛丛丛丛丛

PROBLEMS

IN

ETHICS

ONE of the most common criticisms of philosophy is that it fails to deal with the essential human problems. No doubt, this criticism has some foundation when directed to certain individual thinkers and certain philosophical movements. But nothing so thoroughly discredits it as the strong and persistent interest philosophers in general have taken in the fundamental problems of ethics. In almost all historical periods the literature on ethics has been at least as extensive as that in any other branch of philosophy. Unfortunately, limitations of space make it impossible even to begin to do justice to this vast literature. In this chapter a great number of moral problems—egoism versus altruism and the relationship between religion and ethics, for example— have not been touched upon at all.

TELEOLOGY AND DEONTOLOGY

One primary concern of many moral philosophers has been to explain the relationship between two sets of concepts. On the one hand, there are teleological concepts such as the good, the desirable, and happiness or well-being which have to do with the ultimate and proper goals of human striving. On the other hand, there are deontological concepts such as duty, right conduct, and moral responsibility which relate to the kinds of behavior that may properly elicit moral approval. *Ethical teleologists* hold that the second set of concepts is logically subsidiary to the first: that no behavior may be considered right or worthy of moral approval unless it promotes the good or has desirable consequences. To justify a given act or type of behavior on moral grounds, one must show that it is conducive to the good or promotes human well-being. *Ethical deontologists,* on the contrary, maintain that the concepts of right conduct, duty, and moral responsibility are logically independent of the first set of concepts: that an act or type of behavior could be right even if it were inimical to human well-being. Most of the concrete behavior that deontologists recommend to us as our duty does in fact have humanly desirable consequences; but this is not always or necessarily so, and in no case is behavior right *because* it is conducive to the good.

The difference between teleologists and deontologists may be put differently. According to the teleologists an act is right if and only if it conduces to the good, since the term right conduct, properly understood, *means* conduciveness to the good. According to the deontologist most right conduct does lead to the good, but this is merely a factual generalization about right conduct and one to which there may be exceptions. Right conduct and conduciveness to good are terms with wholly distinct meanings.

The teleological principle has been explicitly held by Aristotle, Epicurus, St. Thomas, and the nineteenth-century utilitarians Jeremy Bentham and John Stuart Mill, but almost all the great classical philosophers subscribed to it, if only implicitly. Moreover, teleology is probably in closer accord than deontology with popular twentieth-century thinking. For example, few persons today are able to sympathize with the contention of Kant, the most famous of the deontologists, that it would be wrong to tell a falsehood even to save a man's life. The concepts of right conduct and conduciveness to human well-being are not, however, so closely linked in philosophical and popular thought as may at first appear. Persons who cannot accept the view that it is wrong to tell a lie to save a man's life might nonetheless agree with Ivan Karamasov (in Dostoievsky's novel *The Brothers Karamasov*) that it would be wrong to purchase the salvation of mankind at the expense of eternal torment for a single innocent child. If God were to offer mankind such a bargain, a person of "good moral character" would be outraged at the very idea of being confronted with the choice.

What, then, is the deontologist's alternative to a definition of right conduct as conduct conducive to the good? And what can be said for or against this alternative? Before discussing these questions it will be helpful to make a few distinctions. One of these is between objective right and subjective right, a distinction employed by philosophers in both camps. Its concrete use by the utilitarians will serve as an illustration. According to utilitarianism, the ultimate good is best expressed by the formula "the greatest happiness of the greatest number." Thus, to say that a particular act or a specific kind of act such as truth-telling or promise-keeping is *objectively right* is to say simply that it does in fact promote the greatest happiness of the greatest number. It is clear, however, that a moral agent could be mistaken in his beliefs about what promotes the greatest happiness and that one ought to do what one believes to be right even though he may be mistaken. (As St. Thomas said, "even an erring conscience binds.") It is also clear that an act leading to the greatest happiness of the greatest number may be performed not only from morally desirable motives but also from morally neutral or morally undesirable motives. A mother, for instance, might give her child to a stranger with the sole intent of abandoning him and by so doing promote the best interests of all concerned. Nonetheless, the act would not be morally commendable. Finally, many acts which would lead to the greatest happiness if performed cannot be performed because of limits on human freedom. To say, therefore, that an act is *subjectively right* is to say that the agent believes the act to be objectively right, that the act is performed from morally acceptable motives, and that the agent is free to perform it. This definition of subjective right can be applied without modification to nonutilitarian as well as to utilitarian theories. The definition of objective right, however, varies from one theory to another depending upon the criterion of right conduct employed.

A second distinction we shall find helpful is the one between a particular act or course of behavior and a general type, class, or kind of behavior. Although there is nothing subtle about this distinction, it must be made fully explicit, since it is essential to an understanding of deontological ethics and plays a role even in utilitarian and other teleological theories. In these latter theories the formal definition of objective right is the same whether it be a question of a particular act or a class of acts—whether we are evaluating the concrete behavior of a given individual in a given situation or a general moral rule relating to a kind of behavior that might be performed by anyone. A particular act is justified by showing that it is conducive to the good, and a moral rule enjoining a certain kind of behavior is justified in the same way. Since, however, a given concrete act may be an instance of several different kinds of behavior, conforming perhaps to one moral rule while violating another, it does not follow that an act is objectively right merely because it conforms to some one moral rule. Thus, teleologists tend to regard moral rules as rules of thumb. In general, it is best to tell the truth because in general telling the truth leads to the good. In general, it is best to do what is necessary to save a man's life because in general this too leads to the good. But in any concrete instance of choice, these rules may conflict, and one will be obliged to violate at least one of them. If the only way to save a man's life is to tell a lie, one is obliged to tell a lie. It must not be thought, however, that the teleologist demands that every choice be preceded by lengthy deliberation. Moral rules may be only rules of thumb, but most of them reflect the collective wisdom of past human experience, and unless they conflict, most teleologists regard the fact of their existence as a sufficiently good reason for following them.

With these distinctions in mind we can proceed to a discussion of deontological ethics. The first thing to note is that deontologists claim that what makes a particular act objectively right is its conformity to moral rule, not its conduciveness to good. Second, deontologists tend strongly to the view that a particular act is subjectively right only if it is inspired by respect for moral rule or performed from the motive of duty. Kant was especially rigorous in this respect. According to him benevolence or love of one's fellow man is a morally neutral motive; an act inspired solely by this motive is morally worthless.

Deontologists have been much perplexed by the problem of deciding how one should act when moral rules conflict. Kant had very little to say about this and seemed to suggest that moral rules cannot conflict. The best known twentieth-century deontologist, W. D. Ross, says that in a case of conflict, one must decide by intuition which rule will prevail. No deontologist allows considerations of human weal or woe to be decisive in such cases.

Deontologists are also in disagreement on the justification of moral rules. A number of twentieth-century Anglo-American philosophers tend toward a position known as *rule utilitarianism,* which incorporates the deontologist view with respect to the objective and subjective rightness of particular acts while borrowing the utilitarian view regarding the justification of moral rules. A particular act is objectively right if it accords with a moral rule, and subjectively right if performed out of respect for the moral rule. Moral rules themselves, however, can be shown to be objectively right only by showing that they have a tendency to promote the greatest happiness of the greatest number. W. D. Ross, on the other hand, appeals to intuition in order to justify moral rules, just as he appealed to intuition to decide how one ought to behave in the event of a conflict between moral rules.

Kant's position with respect to the justification of moral rules is more complex. According to Kant all imperative statements, i.e., statements commanding or recommending a certain act or kind of behavior, may be classified as either hypothetical or categorical. A hypothetical imperative, such as will be found in instructions indicating the proper usage of some mechanical gadget, is one which recommends, either explicitly or implicitly, a course of behavior as a means to an end. The obvious intent is that one ought to follow the instructions in order that the gadget function properly. Categorical imperatives, on the contrary, command or recommend a course of behavior regardless of consequences. For Kant, as for all deontologists, moral rules are categorical rather than hypothetical imperatives; he does not, however, justify moral rules by an appeal to intuition, as does Ross, nor by an appeal to consequences, as do the rule utilitarians. Kant contends that specific rules such as truthtelling and promise-keeping are valid moral rules with a genuinely categorical character because they derive from a single and supreme categorical imperative.

Kant gives three formulations of this supreme categorical imperative and insists upon their equivalence. The one that most commentators find clearest and the only one to be discussed here is as follows: Always act so that you may will the maxim of your action to be a universal law. As ordinarily interpreted, this supreme categorical imperative implies that if we can will the universal adoption of a given maxim or principle of behavior, then it is a valid moral rule, and that if the maxim or rule which inspires a specific act cannot be willed as a universal law the act is objectively wrong.

By way of illustration Kant considers the case of a man who, having made a promise, finds that it is in his interest to break it. If he does break the promise, the maxim, principle, or rule guiding his behavior is: Break promises whenever it is in your interest to do so. But, says Kant, this maxim cannot be a genuine moral rule because it cannot be willed as a universal law.

Kant never made clear precisely what he meant by "being able to will" or "being unable to will" the adoption of a maxim as a universal law. In the case of the maxim "Break promises whenever it is in your interest to do so," the impossibility seems to be logical. A promise, it is said, is by definition a pledge to do something regardless of adverse effects on the agent. To urge that promises be broken whenever this is in the interests of the agents is therefore tantamount to urging someone to make promises that are not promises. However, many acts, such as suicide, which Kant regards as objectively wrong, are often inspired by maxims that can logically be willed as universal laws. It is not, for instance, logically impossible to will that everybody who can reasonably anticipate nothing but a few extra weeks of acute suffering commit suicide. If there is an impossibility in willing the universal adoption of a maxim such as this, it must be psychological rather than logical. And if the impossibility is psychological, it is difficult to see why it should be thus impossible unless it contravenes human desires. Indeed, a close examination of the passages in which Kant discusses the justification of moral rules gives support to John Stuart Mill's claim that despite his disclaimers Kant himself surreptitiously appealed to consequences whenever he tried to justify a moral rule.

Although questions concerning the justification of moral rules are of the utmost interest theoretically, moral philosophers, be they teleologists or deontologists, recommend roughly the same general rules of conduct. In practice the clash between teleologist and deontologist most often occurs at the level of specific acts, the question being whether an act in accordance with a moral rule but detrimental in terms of its consequences ought or ought not to be performed. No one, of course, denies that subjecting an innocent child to eternal torment is an evil. If, however, by making an exception to the moral rules which condemn such an act one can produce a good sufficient to offset this evil, and if there is no other way of offsetting it, the consistent teleologist will recommend that the rules be violated whereas the consistent deontologist will uphold them.

Fortunately, situations calling for a choice of this kind are relatively limited. Most clear-cut instances, like the example cited, are purely hypothetical. In fact, teleologists have sometimes argued that in real life they simply do not occur. Be that as it may, in actual experience there are situations which at least seem to be of this kind. Stalin, for instance, believed that he had a forced choice between the extermination of millions of kulaks, many of whom he recognized to be subjectively innocent of any wrongdoing, or the perpetuation of an agricultural crisis producing widespread famine and the death of an even greater number of Russian citizens. In this he may well have been wrong; Khrushchev is credited with having said that Stalin put the cause of the revolution back by some twenty years as a result of his policy on this and other questions. If, however, the situation was as Stalin believed it to be, was he wrong to liquidate the kulaks? Given this assumption, the strict teleologist is obliged to condone Stalin's policy whereas the strict deontologist would have to condemn it. For the teleologist Stalin would have been confronted by a choice between two evils, and the only acceptable course of action was that leading to the lesser evil. The deontologist, however, argues that no one has the moral right to assume responsibility for the death of a single innocent being no matter what good may thereby be accomplished or what evil may thereby be eliminated. The following considerations bear upon this issue:

First, in determining the consequences of his acts the individual is obliged to rely upon generalizations from past experience. But, a rule utilitarian might argue, generalizations from past experience regarding the kinds of conduct with humanly desirable consequences are embodied in moral rules, and the individual who takes it upon himself to substitute his private judgment for the collective wisdom of mankind is likely to defeat his own purpose. Stalin may have thought that by liquidating the kulaks he could add to the sum total of human happiness, but the fact that this contravenes the moral rule that forbids punishment of the innocent should have given him pause. The mere fact that this rule has elicited widespread support constitutes good evidence that he was mistaken. The rejoinder to this argument is that all generalizations from past experience admit of exceptions. If moral rules were infallible guides to behavior, they would never conflict, but in fact, of course, they do. If the situation was as Stalin claimed, he could not have spared the kulaks without being remiss in his duty to prevent severe famine in the cities.

Second, when test cases which exhibit the issue between teleologists and deontologists are posed, the evils resulting from the violation of the moral rule are usually stated more concretely and make a stronger appeal to the imagination than the evils which ensue from observing the moral rule. The famine stricken are anonymous to us, and their suffering and death seem more remote than the suffering and death of the kulaks, whose fate is a matter of human decree. Similarly, the eternal torment of the innocent child, which follows fatally and inevitably upon acceptance of God's hypothetical bargain, holds the center of our interest; we tend to overlook the torments of the unsaved that could be avoided at the child's expense. When this distorting imaginative focus is taken into account, teleology gains in credibility.

Third, the moral rule to prevent suffering ranks high in almost everybody's hierarchy of moral duties. In general, a person capable of making and executing a decision that involves suffering for others is somehow considered lacking in good moral character. President Truman's remark that his decision to bomb Hiroshima did not cost him a night's sleep probably did more damage to his reputation than the decision itself. Yet, if the bombing of Hiroshima was the lesser of two evils and if the evidence for this was so overwhelming as to leave no reasonable doubt, then Truman's ability to execute his choice without emotional crisis would seem to be meritorious. One does not admire a doctor who faints at the sight of blood, a surgeon whose hand trembles for fear of causing his patient pain, or a military commander who risks the loss of a division because he cannot bear to be responsible for the loss of a battalion. In most cases what is needed is more, not less, compassion—more, not less, reluctance to inflict pain. But this ought not to blind us to the fact that there are situations where compassion may be excessive or misdirected.

Fourth, adherence to moral rule is so much a part of our common-sense notion of right that we are sometimes tempted to define a right act as one in accord with moral rule. If, however, a right act is so defined, the substantive issues that divide teleologists and deontologists will not thereby magically disappear. They will simply assume a new linguistic guise. The question "Is it right to violate a moral rule when adherence to the rule would have undesirable consequences?" will be transformed into the question "Should we do what is right even though the consequences are undesirable?"

THE GOOD

The term *good* has a very wide usage. Here, our concern will be with what are often called *intrinsic goods,* or things desirable in and of themselves, as opposed to *instrumental goods,* or things that are valuable because they serve as means to what is intrinsically good. Although this distinction is conceptually sound, most concrete goods are valuable both intrinsically and instrumentally. Everyone agrees that individual happiness is an intrinsic good, but it is also often regarded as an instrumental good, since the happiness of one individual is likely to promote the happiness of others. Surgery is an example of a purely instrumental good, but the number of such pure examples is very small; for unless an instrumental good is positively painful or otherwise disagreeable, we usually come in time to value it for itself. The classic example of a primarily instrumental good that comes in time to be valued for itself is money. Even teleologists, who might be expected to classify right conduct as an instrumental good, usually insist that the performance of duty is, for a person of moral character, an intrinsic as well as an instrumental good. To the extent that the discharge of our duties involves painful sacrifice, duty is an instrumental good to be performed for the sake of some future benefit. But many persons experience a sense of pride and self-satisfaction in doing their duty, and to this extent right conduct is an intrinsic good.

A list of goods which people find intrinsically valuable would include games of chess, beautiful landscapes, well-prepared meals, interesting books, the performance of our duties, love affairs, friendship, travel, leisure, mystic experiences, creative work, and countless other things. Although classical philosophers have frequently sought and claimed to find some trait or characteristic common to all concrete intrinsic goods, most contemporary philosophers are convinced that no such property exists. They would not object to its being said that all intrinsic goods are elements in human happiness or well-being, but they would probably point out that these terms as conventionally employed are so vague that to say something is an element in happiness or well-being is only another way of saying that it is intrinsically good or desirable in itself.

In order to avoid the imprecision of ordinary usage some teleologists have proposed definitions of happiness. One such definition was offered by Aristotle, who said that happiness consists in the exercise of our native faculties, or in activity in accordance with human nature. This definition was taken over by St. Thomas Aquinas and is still often found in the literature of contemporary neo-Thomists. Philosophers who accept this concept of happiness are often called *eudemonists*. A second and even more influential definition of happiness is that of a group of philosophers known as *hedonists*, who say that happiness consists in pleasure. Epicurus and John Stuart Mill were both hedonists. Objections can be made to both definitions, however. Aristotle's definition presupposes that all men are endowed with the same faculties and derive satisfaction from the pursuit of the same goals—a presupposition which has been widely contested in the nineteenth and twentieth centuries. An objection against the hedonists is that many intrinsic goods, e.g., the experience of doing one's duty or the experience of creative work, cannot be called pleasures unless the term pleasure is used as a synonym for "element in human happiness or well-being."

The twentieth-century English philosopher G. E. Moore was one of the last to claim that all intrinsic goods possess a common property. Although his position on this issue has been even more everwhelmingly rejected than that of Aristotle and the hedonists, Moore raised an interesting problem which has continued to preoccupy Anglo-American philosophers. In order to understand Moore, it is necessary to note his distinction between natural and nonnatural properties. A natural property is either a property, like yellow, that is known by the physical senses, or a property, like pleasantness, that is known by simple introspection. A nonnatural property, on the other hand, is one whose existence can be established only by the use of a special intuitive faculty. Moore's position is that the property common to all instances of intrinsic good is of the nonnatural variety. His argument is as follows. If concrete instances of intrinsic good did not have a common property, it would be impossible to understand why we use a single term to refer to them. A class of physical objects is yellow because every member of that class has the property of yellowness; in the same way, a class of objects is good because every member of that class has the property of goodness. This common property cannot, however, be a natural property. If the term good denoted a natural property, there should be some statement of the form "x is good," where x is replaced by the name of a natural property, that everyone would immediately recognize to be true as a simple matter of definition. But no such statement exists. Substitute for x the name of any natural property (pleasure, activity in accordance with human nature, etc.); the statement that results is not true by definition. One can always ask "But is this really what I mean by good?" From these premises Moore's conclusion immediately follows. Since "good" denotes a property, but not a natural property, and since all properties must be either natural or nonnatural, it follows that "good" stands for a nonnatural property. This property will be present in every member of the class of things of which intrinsic goodness can properly be predicated. Those who believe that "good" stands for a natural property are guilty of what Moore calls the *naturalistic fallacy*.

Moore's argument has been challenged by a group of philosophers known as *emotivists,* because of a distinction they draw between descriptive and emotive terms. An *emotive term* is one used to indicate an attitude of favor or disfavor toward that which the term denotes; a *descriptive term* is one used to describe the objects it denotes. According to the emotivists, terms like good and bad are primarily emotive; therefore, the things denoted by these terms need have no property in common other than that of eliciting the favor or disfavor of those who use them. If the term good is commonly used to refer to such diverse things as friendship, beautiful landscapes, and well-prepared meals, it is only because most people approve of these things. Similarly, if the term bad is often used to denote pain, ugliness, and disharmony, it is only because most people have an aversion to them. There is no reason to suppose that such diverse things have any other property in common. In view of the fact that individuals often have different attitudes toward similar or identical objects this is even unlikely.

A second group of philosophers known as *linguistic analysts* have also criticized Moore. They accept the emotivist distinction between descriptive and emotive terms and concur in regarding terms like good and bad as emotive. However, they reject the view that these terms are *primarily* emotive. The typical emotivist contends, for example, that if a person happened to be highly masochistic, there could be no proper logical or linguistic grounds for objecting if he said, "Pain is good." The fact that a person has a favorable attitude toward pain is sufficient to justify his using the term good to denote it. The linguistic analysts, however, hold the view that the descriptive meaning of terms like good and bad is as essential as their emotive meaning. To use them properly one must carefully consider both aspects of their meaning. The emotive aspect is strong enough that we would not be at a complete loss if somebody said, "Pain is good." The sentence, however, clearly involves a disrespect for the conventional descriptive meaning of the term good as embodied in ordinary rules of English usage.

This does not mean that all the things conventionally described as good in correct English usage have a common property. It is true that many descriptive terms, especially technical terms in the highly developed sciences, are employed to refer to well-defined classes of objects having one or more common properties. But there are many purely descriptive terms, especially those with a long history of popular usage, of which this is not true. And it is almost never the case that objects denoted by the descriptive aspects of emotive terms share any single property. Ordinarily, they will only have what is called a "family resemblance." Every object in the group will resemble others in the group in at least one respect, but there is no one point of resemblance for all members. A term for such a group of objects will tend to evoke in the mind of the user the various properties or points of resemblance which predominate in the group. But which of these properties will be evoked on a given occasion and which may properly be used to justify use of the term on that occasion will depend upon the context or circumstances. None of these properties is both a necessary and a sufficient condition for employing the term in question.

Consider more specifically the word good. As noted above, this term is used to refer to a diversity of things, many of which have the property of affording pleasure. It is probable that more good things resemble one another in this respect than in any other. But pleasantness is neither a necessary condition of something's being good, since some good things do not afford pleasure, nor a sufficient condition, since some pleasant things are not good. Good things are alike only in the way that members of the same family are often alike. There is no feature or characteristic common to them all, but there is some set of features which each member of the family possesses in sufficient number to permit us to recognize him as a member. To distinguish between properties of this kind and properties which belong to every member of a given class, analytic philosophers often use the expressions *meaning criteria* and *defining properties,* respectively.

Both the emotivists and the linguistic analysts have improved our understanding of the ways in which value terms are in fact employed. But it is doubtful that the classical philosophers were totally unaware that value terms have emotive as well as descriptive meanings or that their descriptive meanings in ordinary discourse are usually governed by complex medleys of meaning criteria that fall short of being genuine defining properties. In any case, the great difference between these philosophers, on the one hand, and classical moral philosophers, on the other, is largely one of approach and intent. Linguistic analysts are satisfied to sort out, often laboriously and piecemeal, the meaning criteria of moral terms, but the classical philosophers sought to improve upon popular usage by giving these terms clearer descriptive meanings. The emotivist is usually content to demonstrate that good is an emotive term reflecting attitudes of favor, but the classical philosophers sought to determine what attitudes of favor can be rationally justified. The fact that we approve of something and consequently call it "good" is worth making explicit. But the crucial problem in traditional moral philosophy was to determine what things are *worthy* of our approval and may therefore *properly* be called good.

These relatively modest ambitions of most contemporary moral philosophers are largely due to their belief that rationally defensible definitions of "good" are impossible to come by. So long as one believed with Aristotle and St. Thomas that all human beings have very much the same aspirations and that these aspirations are hierarchically organized, the problem of finding a rational definition of good did not seem so formidable. Aristotle believed that all men are so constituted by their nature or essence that they derive the greatest satisfaction in the exercise of their native capacities, the highest of which is intellectual contemplation, and that inferior capacities should be subordinated to it. St. Thomas believed that all men aspire to salvation as the highest good and that inferior values may be judged by their aptitude to promote salvation.

In the last hundred years, however, the belief in a nature or essence common to all men disposing each to aspire to the same ends has been replaced by the belief that individual desires are profoundly conditioned by history, culture, temperament, and education. In consequence, there can be no definition of good that applies universally to all men. At the same time the belief in a highest good to which all others are subordinate has come into disrepute. Instead of thinking of the individual human personality as a neatly organized system of desires, we tend to regard it, in the fashion of Freud, as the scene of conflict between opposing forces. Goods are a heterogeneous lot among which we are obliged to make radical choices; they cannot be harmonized simply by subordinating the inferior to the superior and moderating the excessive claims of the former.

The consequence of this new intellectual climate is a widespread tendency to minimize the role of reason in evaluating goods. We must, say the analysts and the emotivists, acknowledge the heterogeneity of goods and frankly admit their ultimate dependence upon individual and cultural conditioning. Having done so, we will recognize the vanity of older ambitions. We can analyze the actual uses of the term good and observe what individuals or groups actually do desire. Beyond this we cannot reasonably go.

Except for the neo-Thomists who cling to the traditional point of view, the pragmatists, most notably John Dewey, are the only sizable group of twentieth-century philosophers to challenge these pessimistic conclusions about the role of reason in ethics. Dewey accepts, even insists upon, the contemporary view of the human personality as a product of diverse factors such as temperament, historical circumstances, and cultural conditioning. He also grants, again even insists upon, the diversity of individual and cultural values. Both the notion of a universal good and that of a highest good to which other goods must be subordinated are foreign to Dewey's positive theory of value. In fact, he regards these notions as serious impediments to individual well-being and social progress. But, he says, if these considerations have led us to deny reason's competence to evaluate concrete goods, this is only because we misunderstand reason's nature and function. Reason, properly understood, is not a faculty for discerning essences or universals. There are no essences or universals; the belief that there are was the great mistake of classical philosophers. Nor is systematic classification an essential part of rational understanding. The principal role of reason, or *intelligence* as Dewey prefers to say, is the resolution of concrete conflicts. To recognize that the values of a given individual or group conflict is not to undermine reason but rather to indicate its task. No doubt, individuals and cultures are often subject to unfavorable forces or placed in difficult situations which reason cannot modify in a fully satisfactory way. But intelligence is the only reliable means of accomplishing whatever can be accomplished, and nothing so stands in the way of progress as unjustified pessimism with regard to the efficacy of reason resulting from classical misconceptions about its true role.

The distinction between the desired and the desirable—between that which men value and that which is worthy of being valued, between that which men call good and that which ought properly to be called good—loses none of its validity and remains no less susceptible to rational discrimination because we abandon the idea of a universal and a highest good. If men could pursue without effort or strife all the ends which they envisage with favor and if the achievement of any one actually desired goal never conflicted with the achievement of other actually desired goals, these distinctions would be unnecessary and intelligence would have no role in the moral life. But value conflicts are a fact of life; and the role of reason is to resolve or mitigate these conflicts by exploring the various ways in which the goals we set for ourselves may be achieved and tracing the consequences to which their achievement leads. The distinction between the desired and the desirable, the valued and the valuable, the illusory good and the genuine good thus corresponds with the distinction between two kinds of ends-in-view: on the one hand, ends-in-view pursued in ignorance of the various means by which they may be realized and of the consequences to which their realization leads and, on the other hand, ends-in-view pursued with full knowledge of these factors.

Intelligence is, of course, fallible, and judgments of value can be no more certain than judgments of empirical fact. Moreover, what intelligence reveals to be concretely desirable for one individual or group will often be undesirable for another. Finally, since intelligence forbids us to pursue utopian ideals, concrete ends-in-view will never be desirable in every respect. These are all understandable sources of distress, especially to those who are haunted by the traditional ivory-tower ideals of absolute certainty, universality, and unending happiness. But by focusing our attention upon what is desirable for individuals and groups rather than upon what is desirable for the human species, by abandoning the ancient philosophical quest for a highest good that may serve as an infallible measure of all lesser values, and by rejecting utopian ideals in favor of practically achievable goals, we substitute problems which reason can properly manage for problems with which reason—even as traditionally conceived—cannot adequately cope. And in doing so, we do not obliterate the distinction between the desired and the desirable. On the contrary, we discover its rational principle and render it intelligible.

MORAL RESPONSIBILITY

Morally responsible behavior is usually defined in contemporary philosophy as behavior for which the agent may legitimately be praised or blamed. So defined, the concept of moral responsibility is closely related to the concept of subjective right and wrong. This may best be seen by considering a case in which an objectively wrong act has been performed. If one holds the agent morally responsible and blames him, the agent will typically have recourse to one of three types of defense: first, he may claim ignorance; second, he may claim that the act was performed from morally acceptable motives; and third, he may claim to have been compelled to act as he did. "I didn't know." "I meant well." "I couldn't do otherwise." If we feel that any one of these defenses is legitimate, we will tend to withdraw or mitigate our censure.

The problem of this section may thus be stated in three roughly similar but successively more concrete ways. When is an agent morally responsible for his behavior? Under what circumstances may we legitimately blame an agent for objectively wrong behavior? To what extent are ignorance, good motives, and constraint legitimate excuses for wrongdoing?

The person who is ignorant of the nature of a particular act can never be held directly responsible for it. He may, however, be held indirectly responsible if his intelligence and background are such that he could have known what he was doing had he taken due care. On this general statement of principle there is no serious disagreement. Nonetheless, beliefs with respect to the kind and extent of knowledge demanded by morality differ greatly. Deontologists usually hold that to be a person of moral stature relatively little is required in the way of knowledge. It suffices that one know the moral rules and be able to recognize whether an act is or is not in accord with them. Teleologists, on the other hand, are often very demanding. They usually insist that the individual acquire relatively extensive knowledge of the psychological and social consequences of his behavior. Pragmatists especially have stressed the culpability of ignorance.

The question of good motives and moral responsibility is often allied with the question of ignorance and moral responsibility. It sometimes happens that persons who stress the importance of knowledge in the moral life do so to the detriment of good motives. The road to hell, it has been said, is paved with good intentions. If President Truman is to be faulted for Hiroshima, it is not because he chose what he considered to be the lesser of two evils, but rather because he did not give the question sufficient rational consideration and made a serious error of judgment. On the other hand, those who stress the value of good motives sometimes tend to deprecate intelligence and knowledge. This is especially the case among those who conceive of morality as essentially a matter of overcoming temptation by an effort of will. Most philosophers, however, tend to value both factors and would berate anyone seriously lacking in either.

But what are good moral motives? What character traits must a man possess if he aspires to a moral life? Kant emphasized respect for the moral law and a tendency to equate one's worth or dignity as a human being with one's capacity to observe the moral commands of practical reason. Mill and many other utilitarians considered benevolence, the tendency to be disturbed by the sufferings of others and to rejoice in their well-being, the supreme moral virtue. Still others accord a high place to respect for the beliefs of our fellow men and a tendency to experience shame when confronted by their disapprobation. Since moral education proceeds largely by way of shaming individuals into an observance of conventional moral rules, it is not surprising that "a decent regard for the opinions of mankind" and responsiveness to the disapproval of others should be valued. Philosophers, however, have often found this trait suspect—partly because they tend to share Socrates' disdain for "the opinions of the many," and partly because they feel that the spring of moral action ought to lie within rather than outside the individual personality. In any case, most of us do, though in different degrees, mitigate censure for an act we believe to be objectively wrong if it has been inspired by any one of these three motives.

The remaining problem to be discussed is constraint or absence of freedom insofar as it bears upon moral responsibility and subjective right. Everybody agrees that no one can be morally responsible for an act or properly blamed for it unless the act was freely performed. A freely performed act has, however, been defined in two different ways. For some, it is an act of which the agent is the ultimate cause. If, they say, an individual has been caused or determined by heredity or environment to choose an act, the act is not freely performed and the agent cannot be held responsible for it. Those who accept this view of freedom but deny that all choices are determined, thus allowing a place for what they consider genuine freedom and moral responsibility, are called *libertarians.*

According to the second position, of which David Hume was the first great advocate, the term freedom as properly employed in moral discourse signifies the absence of compulsion or constraint, not the absence of determinism.

Definitions of compulsion when used in this context have taken a variety of forms, but the most common is as follows: An individual is compelled if, though wanting or having chosen to do something, he nonetheless finds it impossible or difficult to do it. It is almost unnecessary to point out that the obstacles which prevent us from acting out our desires or choices are of many different kinds and that compulsion is often a matter of degree. The point is that our freedom and moral responsibility are both proportioned to the ease or difficulty we experience in trying to execute our desires or choices. If it is totally impossible to execute a choice, we are in no sense free to do so and thus are not morally responsible for inaction. If, on the other hand, we are able to execute a choice but only with effort and sacrifice, the degree of our freedom and moral responsibility will be in proportion to the effort and sacrifice required.

Where compulsion is physical and total, the application of this criterion is relatively easy. No one would think of blaming a hopeless cripple for failure to save a drowning child. Where, by contrast, the obstacles that stand in the way of executing a choice are psychological or the compulsion less than total, where the problem in executing choice is not the fact of physical disability but the fact that action involves psychological struggle or painful sacrifice, the criterion is far more difficult to apply. It is clear, however, that we do in fact employ it in these cases as well as in the case of total physical disability. Assume that two persons both owe a debt to a third and that the debt has come due. Assume further that the debts are in the same amount and that either man's failure to pay would have the same consequences. Objectively, either man's failure to pay would be equally wrong, but subjectively this need not be the case. If one of the debtors can repay the debt without any real sacrifice to himself or those who depend upon him, and the other can repay the debt only by depriving himself and his family of basic necessities, certainly the former has a greater moral responsibility. He enjoys sufficient freedom, both financially and morally, to render an excuse in terms of compulsion or constraint ridiculous. The person for whom repayment involves heavy sacrifice, on the other hand, enjoys only a limited freedom. He may desire and even choose to repay the debt, but no doubt he also desires and chooses to buy necessities for himself and family. No matter what he does, therefore, he will be compelled or constrained. At least one of his desires or choices will fail to be executed.

𝕣𝕦

DIRECTIONS

IN TWENTIETH-CENTURY

PHILOSOPHY

ALMOST everybody who is at all familiar with traditional philosophy has been struck by its variety. Even in the Middle Ages, when practically all thinkers adhered to Christian doctrine, several philosophical schools with vastly different outlooks emerged. In the twentieth century, however, philosophy is marked by a diversity without parallel in the historical tradition. Some of this diversity will be evident from the following discussion of four major currents of the twentieth century. But the reader should be aware that there are many more important movements than it was possible to discuss in these few pages. The most prominent of these are phenomenology, a movement founded by the German philosopher Edmund Husserl, and neo-Thomism. The reader should also be aware that many famous twentieth-century philosophers who are not closely identified with any philosophical movement have been passed over. Conspicuous among these are the French thinker Henri Bergson, the Spanish-American philosopher George Santayana, and the English-American philosopher Alfred North Whitehead.

PRAGMATISM

Pragmatism is the only major philosophical movement to have originated in America. Charles Sanders Peirce and William James stated its basic premises in the late nineteenth century. More recently it has had many able exponents, including John Dewey, C. I. Lewis, Herbert Mead, Ernest Nagel, and Justus Buchler. Its fundamental contributions have been a theory of meaning and a theory of truth. The epistemological orientation is basically empiricist.

The term *pragmatism* was coined by Charles Peirce, but the meaning it has assumed in popular discourse derives more directly from the writings of William James. Peirce was himself so dissatisfied with the popular conception of pragmatism that he at one point proposed to call his own philosophy *pragmaticism*, a label he regarded as "sufficiently ugly to be safe from kidnappers." Dewey preferred the term *instrumentalism* and Buchler, the latest of the movement's major representatives, eschews all labels.

The Role of Intelligence. The common root of both the pragmatist theory of meaning and the pragmatist theory of truth is a radically new concept of the role and function of reason, or human intelligence—a concept largely inspired by Darwinian evolutionary theory. In the evolutionary process intelligence first appeared in the lower animals and has reached its highest stage of development in men. Thus, human intelligence is a legacy of animal evolution—not as for Plato, Aristotle, and most traditional philosophers a faculty which sets men entirely apart from other animal species.

Like the lower animals men are born with a number of instincts, or tendencies to react in more or less specific ways to environmental stimuli. In the lowest of animal species these instincts are few. An individual within one of these species survives and prospers only to the extent that the environment is favorable to beings with his limited set of instincts. In the event of unfavorable environmental changes, individuals die young, and in time the species disappears. As one mounts the evolutionary scale, instincts multiply. Individuals are capable of reacting to a larger number of environmental stimuli and in a greater variety of ways. As a result, they are better equipped to survive in the face of environmental change. This development, however, exacts a price. The multiplicity of instincts means that the individual will frequently be confronted with difficult problems of choice, since environmental stimuli will often tend to elicit incompatible types of behavior. A survival instinct, for instance, may dictate one course of behavior while a pleasure instinct dictates another. It is at this point that intelligence emerges, its task being to arbitrate between and to regulate the instincts so as to insure the best possible adjustment to the environment and to ease the discomfort attending painful choice.

In the human species instinctual conflict normally expresses itself in intellectual doubt. Human thinking may thus be regarded as an activity designed to ease the discomfort of doubt. This was Peirce's favorite formulation of the role of reason. Dewey, however, regarded intellectual activity more fundamentally as a means of resolving conflicts, since doubt is merely a symptom of conflict. In either case intelligence is a product of an evolutionary process. Its value lies in the fact that it favors human survival and well-being by helping us adapt to environmental change and by reducing psychological stress.

Like all instrumental goods that are not in themselves disagreeable, intellectual activity may come to be valued for its own sake, and this is much to be desired. But a man who persistently employs his intellectual faculties in idle speculation, disdaining reason's role as a means to the fulfillment of his animal nature, is simply perverse. God's thinking may be a "thinking on thinking," as Aristotle said, but Aristotle was profoundly mistaken in urging men to imitate divinity.

The tools of the intellect are, of course, ideas, and the intellect is not likely to fulfill its role unless its ideas are clear and true. But how can we make our ideas clear? How can we know which of the propositions that solicit our belief are true? These are the basic problems of pragmatist epistemology, and the answers to these problems are to be found respectively in the pragmatist theory of meaning and the pragmatist theory of truth.

Theory of Meaning. In a well-known article entitled "How to Make Our Ideas Clear" (first published in 1878 and often considered a kind of pragmatist manifesto), Peirce proposed a criterion for testing the meaningfulness of any proposition: What activity would you have to undertake and what observations would have to result from this activity before you would be prepared to pronounce the proposition true? If you can conceive of any course of action having observable consequences that would verify it, then the proposition is meaningful; if you cannot, it is meaningless. As an illustration of a meaningful proposition, Peirce invites us to consider a statement of the form "x is harder than y." What does it mean? Peirce answers: x is harder than y means that if you rub x against y you will observe that y has a scratch whereas x emerges from the encounter unmarred. As an example of a meaningless proposition Peirce proposes: "The wine and the wafer in the sacrament of the mass are the blood and flesh of Christ." There is, he says, no experimental test or observable fact of experience which could conceivably verify the truth of this proposition. Thus, it is meaningless.

One of the consequences of Peirce's criterion of meaningfulness is that any two sentences, however different their verbal form, will have precisely the same meaning if the experimental procedures and results required to verify them are the same. The criterion thus serves as a means of identifying all purely verbal disputes.

Theory of Truth. In the light of the pragmatist theory of meaning, a part of the pragmatist theory of truth can be stated very briefly. A proposition is true only if the verifying operations included in the elaboration of its meaning have the observable results predicted. Obviously, however, a theory of truth formulated wholly in terms of the pragmatist theory of meaning could not be satisfactory, since the latter itself presupposes a theory of truth.

The pragmatist theory of truth starts from the premise that a true proposition is one worthy of belief. This premise constitutes a formal and abstract definition of truth, but it does not take us very far. What makes a proposition worthy of belief? The pragmatists answer that a proposition is worthy of belief if and only if belief in that proposition promotes human well-being, either by helping us to adapt to the environment or by resolving internal conflicts. Once again, however, the answer is too formal and abstract. We still want to know what makes belief in a proposition conducive to well-being.

Unfortunately, the answers pragmatists have given to this last question are not always clear and are not always fully in accord with one another. William James was particularly confused on this issue, and many careless statements in his writings have given rise to the popular notion that pragmatists consider any proposition true if believing it affords some momentary psychological comfort or promotes the achievement of some crude, short-range goal. This popular interpretation is not, however, even a faithful statement of James's own views and is completely at odds with the views of other pragmatists. All pragmatists, including James, insist that no one has the right to accept a proposition as true simply because it would be painful to reject it or because belief in it leads to some immediate advantage. If a proposition is to count as true, it must promote our long-range, not our short-range, advantage, and the fulfillment of our long-range interests frequently requires painful sacrifice in the way of belief, as in all other things. A belief, says Peirce, is not only a feeling but also a habit of action. To believe that fire burns is to possess the habit of avoiding direct contact with fire. To suspend that belief and put one's faith in the proposition that fire does not burn in order to allay anxiety if one's house catches fire may be to one's momentary advantage but it is certainly not in one's best long-range interest.

Probably the clearest answer to this question is that of Dewey, who said that only those propositions are worthy of belief which have the sanction of science or intelligent common sense. To adapt to our environment and to resolve internal conflict, we must be able to anticipate the future and to estimate the consequences of alternative lines of conduct. It is only on this condition that we can hope to survive in the face of rapid change and, so far as it is humanly possible, to eliminate painful conflict. But the scientific method, which is essentially a refinement of intelligent common sense, is the one and only method mankind has devised that successfully permits prediction and control of the future course of events. Those who accept as worthy of belief propositions whose sole sanction is authority, or blind faith, or prejudice, or immediate comfort, rejecting the tried and true methods of experimental inquiry, may be lucky enough to avoid acute discomfort. The odds, however, are against even this, and overwhelmingly against their ever knowing the fullest possible measure of well-being.

The import of the pragmatist theory of truth can best be seen by contrasting it with two other theories of truth. The first and oldest is known as the correspondence theory, which was implicit in the thinking of most traditional philosophers, especially the representationalists. According to this theory, a proposition is true if and only if it stands for a reality or actual state of affairs to which it faithfully corresponds. Consider the sentence, "The cat is on the mat." This sentence tends to evoke a picture or image of a particular cat on a mat. If in actuality the cat is on the mat, and if the picture or image the sentence evokes in the mind is a faithful copy or representation of the physical state of affairs, the proposition expressed by that sentence is true. Otherwise, the proposition is false.

The correspondence theory of truth has a great initial appeal, and it should be noted that it is not necessarily inconsistent with the pragmatist theory of truth. A pragmatist could well argue that only those propositions are worthy of belief which correspond to a reality and that it would be humanly undesirable to repose confidence in propositions that do not. As a rule, however, pragmatists criticize the correspondence theory on two related grounds. First, it does not go to the root of the problem, and second, it does not authorize belief in a number of propositions that merit belief. Consider the proposition, "The figure before us has a thousand sides." The image of a thousand-sided figure does not copy or correspond to the reality it supposedly stands for. As Descartes observed, the image of a thousand-sided figure does not significantly differ from the image of a hundred-sided figure. The true meaning of the proposition can only be expressed in a formula specifying operations to be performed and results to be observed. To say that a given figure has a thousand sides is to say that if you counted its sides you would observe that their mathematical sum is a thousand. Consider also propositions relating to atoms. Many of these propositions are worthy of belief, but since nobody can observe physical atoms there is no direct way of knowing whether the pictures or images evoked by atomic theory correspond to reality. Indeed, many scientists insist that the images or pictures (in more contemporary terminology the *models*) associated with atomic theory hinder rather than aid its full understanding and development. The meaning of propositions having to do with atoms must, therefore, be understood in terms of experimental operations and the observable results of these operations.

The second alternative theory of truth is called the coherence theory. It was developed by a number of late nineteenth-century thinkers, most especially the English philosopher Francis Herbert Bradley and the American philosopher Josiah Royce. These thinkers combined a rationalist epistemology with a monistic metaphysics. The ultimate nature of reality, they said, is fully rational and can be discovered by the use of reason alone. At the same time, they argued that every thing is so related to every other thing that the true nature of any single event can be known only when it is viewed from the standpoint of the whole of being. It follows that the measure of any proposition's truth is its coherence or logical consistency with other propositions.

The pragmatists grant that coherence is a useful secondary criterion of truth. If there are two propositions relating to the same state of affairs, the proposition more worthy of belief, other things being equal, is the one which best accords with the main body of well-confirmed propositions to which we already hold. Since, however, the pragmatists reject both rationalism and monism, they cannot agree that coherence is the primary criterion of truth. A proposition about the world cannot even be meaningful, much less true, unless it is anchored to observable facts of experience. And since many facts of nature are ontologically independent of others, many true propositions will also be logically independent of others.

LOGICAL POSITIVISM

Logical positivism was developed in the 1920's by a group of philosophers often referred to as the Vienna Circle. The best known members of the circle are Moritz Schlick and Rudolf Carnap; it also included Otto Neurath, Herbert Feigl, and Gustav Bergmann. The term *logical positivism* itself was coined by Feigl and the American philosopher Albert Blumberg. Ludwig Wittgenstein, who though an Austrian was not closely associated with the Vienna Circle and who later turned his back on positivism, developed independently very similar ideas which he published in his first major work, *Tractatus Logico-Philosophicus*. A. J. Ayer did much to popularize positivism in England, and, owing largely to the fact that many of the Austrian positivists moved to the United States in the 1930's, the movement has flourished in America. Though the movement is still best known as logical positivism, many of its major representatives have come to prefer the label *logical empiricism*.

Like the pragmatists, positivists have been primarily concerned with epistemology. However, whereas pragmatist theory of knowledge has its source in a particular view of man and his relationship to nature, positivism is an outgrowth of reflections on logic and language. Most of the positivists are in fact excellent logicians, and they have made a number of original contributions to the field.

The positivists owe a great deal to David Hume, as do all later empiricists. Hume, it will be remembered, maintained that all meaningful propositions are either empirical and a posteriori, in which case they have to do with "matters of fact," or analytic and a priori, in which case they are concerned with "relationships between ideas." From one point of view positivism may be regarded as an attempt to give this distinction the clearest possible technical formulation and to trace its many ramifications. In approaching this task the positivists introduced what at first appears to be a relatively minor shift of emphasis, but, as it turns out, one with far-reaching consequences. Like many traditional philosophers Hume often talked about the meaning of "ideas." (The pragmatist Peirce was merely following this tradition when he entitled his famous essay "How to Make Our Ideas Clear.") The positivists, however, feel that the term meaning ought to be used primarily for linguistic expressions. Since meanings can only be conveyed by language and since verbal symbols are essential to the successful execution of even very simple forms of thinking, that which we must first be clear about is language. Clear language means clear thinking. Clear thinking without clear language is totally impossible.

One result of this emphasis upon language as the primary bearer of meaning is a redefinition of a priori propositions. Traditionally, an a priori proposition was said to be one whose truth or falsity could be established by reason alone, without appeal to experience. The fact, however, that meaning is predicated of language rather than of ideas and that linguistic symbols are physical entities (marks on paper or sounds produced in the throat) means that in order to establish the truth of an a priori proposition one must know the physical nature of the symbols used to express it and also the ways in which people actually use these physical symbols. For the positivist, therefore, a priori propositions are not propositions whose truth or falsity can be established by reason alone. To know that the proposition expressed by the sentence "All bachelors are unmarried" is true, one must be familiar with the physical symbols appearing in that sentence and the human decisions or conventions that govern the use of these symbols. The significant thing about a priori propositions, the property which defines them and by virtue of which they may properly be distinguished from empirical or factual propositions, is that their truth or falsity can be determined without appeal to nonlinguistic fact. To know that "All bachelors are unmarried" is true, empirical knowledge of the symbols in this sentence and the rules governing their usage suffices. One does not need to know anything about the men we call bachelors.

For positivists, as for empiricists in general, all a priori propositions are analytic and all analytic propositions are a priori. The positivists do not, however, accept Kant's definition of analyticity. They agree that a statement whose predicate is contained in its subject is analytic. But, they point out, the idea of "being contained in" is a spatial metaphor ill suited to the analysis of language and meaning. They also point out that many statements which even Kant would have regarded as analytic do not have the subject-predicate form. For instance, the statement "If John is taller than Henry and Henry taller than Bill, then John is taller than Bill" is clearly analytic. But it does not have a subject-predicate form. For Kant's definition of analyticity, therefore, the positivists substitute one with the advantages of greater clarity and greater generality. According to the positivist definition, a statement is analytic if and only if its contradictory is self-contradictory. For example, the contradictory of "All bachelors are unmarried" is the obviously self-contradictory statement "Some bachelors are married."

When, therefore, the positivist asserts an equivalence between a priori statements and analytic statements, he is not asserting that all statements whose truth can be determined by reason alone are statements whose truth follows from the predicate's being contained in the subject. He is asserting rather that all statements whose truth can be determined by an appeal to linguistic fact alone are statements whose contradictories are self-contradictory.

The positivist criterion of analyticity is allied to Hume's criterion of the unimaginability or inconceivability of the proposition's opposite, but it differs significantly in that it applies to statements rather than to ideas and is formulated in logical rather than psychological terms.

For the Cartesian criteria of indubitability or clarity and distinctness, the positivist has little sympathy. He recognizes that in fact most true analytic or a priori propositions are clearer and more certain than most synthetic, empirical statements, but, he holds, this is not always so. Moreover, Descartes' criteria are too vague, and, like Hume's criterion, they suffer from being couched in psychological rather than logical terms.

Analytic or a priori statements fall into two distinct classes, to which the names *logical statements* and *definitional statements* are sometimes given. As examples of logical statements, consider: "All married men are married" and "Either John is in the library or John is not in the library." In these statements there are two kinds of terms. "Married men," "John," and "in the library," may be called *empirical terms* because they denote empirically describable facts or states of affairs. The other kind of terms, e.g., All, are, Either . . . or, and not, have no empirical content; they do not denote anything at all, much less empirically describable states of affairs. These may be called *logical terms.* The defining property of logical statements is that they can be known to be true or false even though one disregards the meaning of their empirical terms. To put the point somewhat differently, logical statements are statements whose truth or falsity can be determined simply by examining their logical form. "All married men are married," for instance, has the logical form "All AB's are A's"; and a statement having this form is true for that reason alone. Again, "Either John is in the library or John is not in the library" has the form "Either A or not A"; and the statement is true because all statements having this form are true. To know that it is true there is no need to establish the actual whereabouts of John. The statement would be true if John happened to be in a bar, at a movie, or on a baseball field.

Definitional statements, on the other hand, are not analytic or a priori by virtue of their form alone. These statements can be recognized as analytic or a priori only by an examination of the meanings assigned to their empirical terms. As an example of a definitional statement, consider again "All bachelors are unmarried." This statement is analytic, since its contradictory is clearly self-contradictory. It is no less certainly a priori, since the only facts one needs to know to establish its truth are facts about the way in which people use language. But it is not a logical statement, since its logical form, "All A's are B's," does not guarantee its truth. Many statements having this form, e.g., "All men are ten feet tall," are false.

Since definitional statements are true by virtue of the meanings assigned to their empirical terms and since different people or even the same people at different times may assign different meanings to empirical terms, a statement that is definitional for some may not be definitional for others, and a statement that is definitional at one time may not be definitional at another time. The truth of a definitional statement depends upon human choices or conventions regarding the ways in which words are to be used. By using words differently than they have been used in the past we may change an a priori, analytic truth into an a posteriori, synthetic statement, or vice versa. For instance, at one time there was a strong tendency to define "pure water" as water that was merely clear or transparent, thereby rendering the statement "Clear water is always pure water" a definitional truth. Since the time of Pasteur, however, the term pure water has come to mean for most of us water free of germs detrimental to the human organism. And since clear water may nonetheless contain obnoxious germs, the statement "Clear water is always pure water" is no longer always true by definition. As ordinarily interpreted, it is, in fact, a false empirical statement.

That the truth of definitional statements depends on human choices or conventions has long been recognized. Until well along in the nineteenth century, however, it was widely believed that what the positivists call logical statements are true independently of human choice or convention. Statements having the form "All AB's are A's" and "Either A or not A" were thought to express immutable logical principles, lodged so to speak in the order of nature. If a logical statement is true at one time or for one person the same statement uttered at another time or by another person will also be true. The positivists, on the contrary, hold that logical truths, though distinguishable from definitional truths, are nonetheless like them in being products of human choice or convention. Just as definitional truths are established by decisions to use words in certain ways, so too are logical truths. The difference between the two types of statements is that the truth of definitional statements depends upon choices or conventions regarding its empirical terms whereas the truth of logical statements depends entirely upon choices or conventions regarding the use of its logical terms.

If classical philosophers did not see this, it is largely because the conventions regarding the use of logical terms in ordinary language are so widely accepted and serve the ordinary purposes of inquiry so well that it is difficult to imagine an alternative set of rules. A number of nineteenth and twentieth century developments, however, have given support to the positivist view. Chief among these were the appearance of non-Euclidean geometries and the successful use of these geometries by Einstein and others in astral physics. Since non-Euclidean geometries serve even better than Euclidean geometry for the understanding of some aspects of nature, Euclidean geometry could no longer be plausibly regarded as a set of universal and necessary truths inscribed in the nature of things. And since logical truths had long been considered to be of the same or a very similar nature to mathematical truths, logical truths could no longer be plausibly so construed either. (In *Principia Mathematica* Bertrand Russell and Alfred North Whitehead argued that mathematics was only a branch of logic.)

Mathematical and logical systems have thus come to be widely regarded, not as reflections of the ultimate nature of the universe, but rather as sets of man-made symbols to be manipulated in accordance with man-made rules. The value of these systems is not the fidelity with which they picture nature, but rather their pragmatic utility. Euclidean geometry and Aristotelian logic, which Kant still believed to be the only geometry and the only logic conceivable, have lost their privileged status. Other systems of symbols have been invented that are no less useful. How it can be determined which of various possible systems of symbols best serves a specific purpose is a question that will not be dealt with here. It must, however, be noted how admirably the positivist conception of the meaning of logical and mathematical truths solves the long-standing rationalist objections to empiricist epistemology. So long as rationalists and empiricists both held that meaningfulness is predicated primarily of ideas and that words are meaningless unless they stand for ideas, the empiricist could not easily explain mathematical terms such as zero and infinity or logical terms such as All, not, and or. If all our ideas are derived from sense impressions, if the mind has no innate faculty for representing to itself ideas of a higher order than images, then terms of this kind would appear to be meaningless. We saw in Chapter Three how Berkeley struggled with this problem. The positivist has a far easier time of it. Since meaning is predicated of linguistic symbols, for a word to be meaningful it is enough that it be a part of a system of symbols containing rules for its proper usage. It need not stand for an idea at all.

In their analysis of empirical statements the positivists have proposed a criterion of meaningfulness which has come to be called *the verification principle of meaning*. It has been given both a stronger and a weaker formulation. According to the stronger and original formulation, an empirical statement is genuinely meaningful only if its empirical terms stand for directly observable facts or states of affairs. This stronger statement of the principle was almost immediately abandoned by the positivists themselves. As Schlick pointed out, the statement "There are mountains on the side of the moon that cannot be observed from earth" is certainly a meaningful statement, but at the time there were no technical or practical means of directly observing that side of the moon. The weaker version, therefore, asserts that a statement is meaningful only if its empirical terms stand for facts or states of affairs that are either directly or conceivably observable. Although one could not go to the moon and directly observe its surface, even in the 1920's one could conceive of steps to be taken that might eventually result in a direct verifying observation. Sometimes the difference between the stronger and the weaker principle is briefly expressed by saying that a meaningful statement must be verifiable either *in fact* or *in principle*.

The positivist criterion of empirical meaningfulness is similar to the pragmatist criterion as stated by Peirce. It differs from the latter, however, in that it does not require of a meaningful statement that it be possible to specify verifying operations as well as empirical observation. The positivist agrees that in fact most empirically meaningful statements require for their explication a reference to experimental tests. The statement relating to mountains on the far side of the moon is obviously of this kind. Positivists, however, recognize a second class of empirically meaningful statements—statements which are immediately verifiable by a single and infallible perceptual act. A possible example is: "I am now having a sensation of blue." The positivists argue that these statements—sometimes called *protocol statements*—are the basic propositions to which all more complex empirical statements must ultimately be reduced.

The positivists also differ from the pragmatists in the use they make of their theory of meaning. Positivists have used it to discredit the meaningfulness of many statements in traditional metaphysics and ethics. Pragmatists, on the contrary, have usually tried to reinterpret metaphysical and ethical statements in the light of their theory of meaning. Positivists, for instance, usually argue that moral statements are neither a priori nor empirical and consequently meaningless. Pragmatists, on the contrary, usually argue that moral statements are obviously meaningful and that the task of the philosopher is to exhibit their meaningfulness by showing how they relate to experience.

It goes almost without saying that in natural languages such as ordinary English there is considerable vagueness and ambiguity. Many statements which at first appear to be analytic or empirical turn out upon analysis to be neither. Often it is difficult to tell whether any given statement is best classified as analytic or empirical. Moreover, the rules governing the use of logical terms are merely implicit, and it rarely happens that the protocol statements to which the meaning of more complex empirical terms must be reduced are explicitly stated. The positivists have, therefore, set themselves the task of creating an artificial language without any of these defects. This effort is often called the *positivist program.*

ANALYTIC PHILOSOPHY

The term *analytic philosophy* is used in both a wider and a narrower meaning. In its wider meaning, it suggests merely a preoccupation with logic or language and a disdain for highly speculative philosophy, particularly traditional metaphysics. In this wide sense the logical positivists are analytic philosophers, as are Bertrand Russell and G. E. Moore. Employed more narrowly, as in this section, *analytic philosophy* denotes the kind of work done by the later Wittgenstein, J. L. Austin, and Gilbert Ryle. In this narrower sense, the movement is also known as *ordinary language philosophy* or *linguistic analysis.*

Since analytic philosophy is more closely related to logical positivism than to any other philosophical movement, the best introduction to it will be a statement of the way in which the two movements differ. The essential difference is that whereas positivists tend to despair of natural languages and pin their hopes to artificial languages, the analysts maintain that the philosopher's primary job is close analysis of ordinary language. The analytic philosopher grants that the rules governing ordinary usage are often only implicit and that words in ordinary language often have multiple and sometimes even conflicting meanings.

Nonetheless, he believes that making these rules explicit and exposing the confusions resulting from ordinary uses of language can as a rule best be accomplished without recourse to artificial languages. Highly formalized logical reconstructions of the language employed in a given field can sometimes be helpful, especially in the sciences. But in fields such as ethics, aesthetics, philosophy of law and countless others, a less formalized approach is more enlightening. The implicit and informal logic of ordinary language is the cumulative product of a vast human experience. It is, therefore, reasonable to suppose that many of the linguistic puzzles and confusions which positivists attribute to defects of the informal logic embedded in ordinary usage are more properly attributable to a misunderstanding of that logic or an abuse of the rules of ordinary usage. It is also reasonable to suppose that the informal logic of everyday language is better adapted to the multiple purposes of ordinary life than any contrived formal logical scheme one might wish to substitute for it.

Indeed, hasty and premature attempts to formalize and simplify ordinary language for the sake of clarity often defeat their own purpose and cause us to overlook important problems. The positivist's artificial language with its purified logic, for instance, provides a berth only for analytic and empirical statements; all others are declared meaningless and survive in ordinary language only on sufferance. But is it really conducive to clarity to assert that all statements which are neither analytic nor empirical are meaningless? And will not the philosopher who so grandly dismisses these statements risk depriving himself of useful knowledge that only a close scrutiny of ordinary discourse could make available?

It must be noted here that the positivist program is to create a purified language for knowledge claims, not for the whole of ordinary language. It should also be noted that when positivists declare that all nonanalytic and nonempirical statements are meaningless, they usually add a qualification. These statements, they will say, are empirically, cognitively, or literally meaningless. The import of the qualification is simply that nonanalytic and nonempirical statements cannot communicate knowledge. If the politician, or the priest, or the lawyer, or the man in the street find nonanalytic and nonempirical statements useful for their own special purposes, so be it. But as epistemologists or philosophers of science, the positivists have no need of them and are not obliged to undertake their analysis.

But many analysts will challenge this retort. First, in elaborating, explaining, and justifying any artificial language, one must use some ordinary natural language. Moreover, in trying to justify a chosen artificial language it is almost inevitable that one will use statements that are neither analytic nor empirical. Unless, therefore, one understands the informal logic of that language, errors can creep in. Consider the positivist claim that in a purified scientific language all statements must be either analytical or empirical. What is the nature of this claim? If it is analytic, then the assertion that a purified scientific language contains statements that are neither analytic nor empirical should be self-contradictory—which it appears not to be. Is it then empirical? This, too, seems doubtful. What empirically observable facts could conceivably verify it?

Second, positivists tend to lump all literally or descriptively meaningless statements together and to dismiss them with a blanket term such as *emotive*. But the class of scientifically meaningless statements is very large; and although some are primarily emotive, functioning principally to express the speaker's feelings or to arouse feelings in others, many are not. For example, sentences such as "Close the door, please," "I promise to return the book before Friday," and "It is my great honor to introduce to you the speaker of the evening" are not primarily emotive. The first is a simple request. The second constitutes a kind of act. (Analysts often call it a *performatory utterance*.) The third is chiefly a symbol of the speaker's respect for social etiquette. (Statements of this third kind are often called *ceremonial utterances*.) The positivists also give insufficient heed to the fact that a single sentence often serves several functions simultaneously. They want to pigeonhole statements as either literally meaningful or emotive, and if they see that a statement is emotive they tend to overlook its descriptive aspects. This is particularly evident in their penchant for emotivism—which is much too simple and reductionistic a theory of moral language. Moral statements are no doubt emotive. If someone said "x is wrong, but I approve of it," one would be very puzzled. But from the fact that moral statements are emotive, it does not follow that they lack descriptive meaning or that it is impossible to give them a rational justification. If someone says "x is wrong," he ordinarily implies not only that he disapproves of x but also that x has certain empirical features which justify him in calling it "wrong." Of course, as we saw in the last chapter, these features are not, properly speaking, defining properties. There is no single property common to every instance of wrong-doing. Wrong acts have only a family resemblance. Nonetheless, there are empirical or descriptive meaning criteria for the word wrong, and it is important to sort them out.

Thirdly, the positivists' impatience with terms for which there is no precise and conventionally agreed upon set of defining properties tends to vitiate the positivist program itself. Many purely descriptive terms are used to denote objects having only a family resemblance. Terms for which it is only possible to specify a loose set of meaning criteria abound in practically all the sciences. They do not, however, find a place in the purified scientific language the positivists are trying to elaborate. If, therefore, this artificial language is regarded as a logical reconstruction of the sciences in their present stage of development, it will be thoroughly im-poverished and inadequate. If, alternatively, the artificial language is regarded as a tool or instrument to aid the scientist in his task of discovery, it will fail in its purpose. The principal mark of scientific progress is the extent to which vague and loose terms of everyday language are replaced by precise and clearly defined terms. But precise scientific definitions do not precede inquiry; they follow from it. And scientific inquiry often has to begin with an informal analysis of the everyday terms the scientist wishes to elucidate and eventually replace. Unless, therefore, these loose everyday terms are somehow admitted to the artificial language, it is difficult to see how it can help the scientist do his job. If, finally, the artificial language is regarded as the form which scientific lan-guage will assume at some indefinitely deferred future date when everything has been scientifically explained, then the absence of terms without precise definitions is not surprising. But in this case positivism is reduced to the statement of an ideal that will prob-ably never be achieved.

Before we pass to a discussion of existentialism, the reader should be warned against several misunderstandings that might otherwise result from the decision to explain the analytic movement by concentrating upon its critique of positivism. First, although analysts do criticize positivists, the critique of positivism occupies a small place in analytic literature. The principal contributions of the analysts are studies of specific word families ranging over a wide variety of fields. Second, in an effort to bring out the essential differences between analysts and positivists, positivism has been unduly oversimplified. Most of the criticisms of positivism which have here been put to the account of the analysts were made by positivists themselves, often even before the analysts appeared on the scene. The positivists have been remarkably candid in admitting inadequacies in their original theories and have demonstrated a great deal of technical ingenuity in meeting objections. Finally, by focusing upon the differences between positivists and linguistic analysts, we have obscured their common interest in dispelling the puzzles and paradoxes of traditional philosophy by introducing more refined tools of analysis and paying greater attention to language. Many commentators would regard this common interest as the essential characteristic of both movements.

EXISTENTIALISM

In the past philosophers on either side of the English Channel have taken little note of one another. There have, of course, been exceptions. The British empiricists were influenced by Descartes. John Locke had great prestige on the Continent during the period of the Enlightenment. And Hegel was taken up with enthusiasm by many English philosophers at the end of the nineteenth century. Still, English and continental European philosophers generally went their separate ways.

In the twentieth century this traditional indifference has been replaced by mutual incomprehension and actual hostility. Pragmatism had a minor success in Italy, and analytic philosophy has become popular in Scandinavia. In the main, however, twentieth-century continental philosophers disdain the dominant movements in Anglo-American philosophy. The analyst's conception of philosophy strikes them as perverse: the analysis of language is mere philology. The philosopher's true task is to arrive at a just conception of man and a comprehensive account of the world. The positivist program leaves them unmoved. Science, they believe, gives a distorted picture of man and his place in nature. Finally, the pragmatist conception of man as the end product of animal evolution who differs from the lower animals only in being more intelligent is considered to be at best superficial. Contemporary continental philosophers do not agree with Descartes in regarding the lower animals as mindless machines or automata, but they do consider that a chasm separates man from the lower animals.

The disdain of Anglo-American philosophy is particularly evident among the existentialists. Unfortunately, existentialism is a less cohesive movement than those discussed so far, and a brief exposition is likely to be even sketchier and less satisfying. Among the major existentialists are the Dane Søren Kierkegaard, the so-called "father of existentialism" who died in the middle of the nineteenth century; Friedrich Nietzsche, a German philosopher of the late nineteenth century; Martin Heidegger, a twentieth-century German philosopher; and Jean-Paul Sartre, a Frenchman born in 1905. Of these four figures Sartre is the only one to accept the label existentialist. In addition to these major figures, a number of other thinkers have been identified with the movement: Christian philosophers like Gabriel Marcel, Miguel de Unamuno, Léon Chestov, and Nicholas Berdyaev; the Jewish philosopher Martin Buber; the atheists Albert Camus, Merleau-Ponty, and Simone de Beauvoir; and also Karl Jaspers, whom many persons would rank among the major representatives of existentialism.

Although existentialism is a much older movement than one would be led to believe by comment in the popular press, it did not become a major current in the European intellectual climate until after World War II. For many, Jean-Paul Sartre personifies existentialism; through his novels, plays, and occasional articles he has done more than anyone else to bring existentialism to the attention of a large public; in his technical works he has given existentialism one of its most carefully formulated expressions. This section will, therefore, be limited to a brief statement of the main points in Sartre's first major work, *Being and Nothingness*.

The principal concepts of *Being and Nothingness* are consciousness, freedom, and authenticity. Consciousness, or the mere brute fact of human awareness, has long puzzled philosophers, and Sartre does not claim to have solved all aspects of the puzzle. He does not, for instance, claim to know how or why consciousness emerged; this he considers an insoluble problem. Sartre does, however, claim to understand the function of consciousness: to invest being-in-itself with value and meaning.

By *being-in-itself*—or *facticity,* as he also calls it—Sartre understands in the first instance what Kant understood by noumenal being: things as they are prior to and independent of human observation or awareness. Sartre does not agree, however, that man can know nothing of the noumenal world except that it exists. Sartre maintains that there are moments when being-in-itself is revealed to us in its true character. These are moments of anguish when life loses its meaning: when the objects that formerly drew our attention fade into oblivion and the desires that had previously guided our conduct seem vain or petty. In these moments we no longer have an anchor in what Sartre calls technically *the world:* the clearly differentiated and related objects present to consciousness in everyday living. In anguish the world dissolves; once familiar objects of concern suddenly seem strange, and we no longer recognize them for what they were. Nothing is present to consciousness but being-in-itself in all its ugly nudity: a mass of pure matter or solid being altogether meaningless and without value.

This anguished confrontation with the in-itself teaches us that being is alien to man and indifferent to human aspirations. It also leads to a momentous discovery about ourselves. Since being-in-itself is alien, we recoil against it almost instinctively. In doing so, we discover that we have no place to go. There is no soul, no self, no ego, no I into which we can withdraw. Consciousness—or, as Sartre also calls it, *being-for-itself*—is nothing at all except consciousness of being. Were it not for facticity, consciousness would have no object. A consciousness that is not consciousness of something would be a pure nothingness.

Persons who have not known the experience of existential anguish often find it odd that anybody would dare to base his philosophy on it. Is not anguish merely a symptom of neurosis or a momentary psychological disequilibrium induced by fatigue, boredom, or personal crisis? Most persons, however, who know this experience well —and there are far more than those who do not know it usually suspect—value it highly. Just as the religious mystic believes that his experience is a revelation of ultimate truths not available to us in everyday life, so those who experience existential anguish interpret it as an experience with infinitely greater revelatory value than "normal" experiences of life. What, they ask, except pure prejudice leads one to believe that truth is revealed by ordinary everyday experiences? Why should unusual experiences be snares of deception? If truth is as hard to come by as most philosophers think, the contrary hypothesis is at least as reasonable.

We learn through anguish that the only ultimate realities are facticity, or being-in-itself, which is indifferent to human aspirations, and consciousness, or being-for-itself, which requires being-in-itself for its very existence. In doing so we lose the sense of security afforded by traditional views of nature as a created providential order and of man as a substantial soul. But we also lose the world: the milieu of everyday life, the system of objects that previously solicited our attention and interest. And here a question arises. What was this world that dissolved in the experience of anguish? If the only ultimate realities are being-in-itself and consciousness, how can there be a world at all? Being-in-itself, says Sartre, is what it is eternally; except for the inexplicable emergence of consciousness nothing ever happens in or to being-in-itself. Consequently, being-in-itself cannot give rise to the world. The world must, then, arise through consciousness. But consciousness, as we know, is a purely derivative and marginal being that depends upon being-in-itself for its very existence. How can it give rise to the world? Sartre answers that consciousness gives rise to the world because it lies in the very nature of consciousness freely to create values and to confer upon being-in-itself an interpretation consistent with its choice of values. The world is thus the in-itself as seen or known by a consciousness that has freely projected a set of personal values or goals.

Just as Sartre's concept of being-in-itself corresponds roughly to Kant's concept of the noumenal world, so Sartre's concept of the world corresponds roughly to Kant's concept of phenomenal being.

There are, however, important differences. For Kant the phenomenal world is a product of universal and necessary structures of all human consciousness. There is only one phenomenal world, and it does not lie within the power of either the individual or the race to choose it. For Sartre, however, every individual has his own world, and his world exists by virtue of personal choice. There is no universal a priori structure of consciousness, no common human nature, no native set of desires shared by all men that dispose us to project one kind of values to the exclusion of others or to give being-in-itself one kind of meaning rather than another. Each individual is absolutely free.

This freedom is not, however, an unmixed blessing. Since the individual is absolutely free to choose his world, he is absolutely responsible for the world in which he lives. Being-in-itself did not cause him to choose it. If, therefore, he made a bad choice he cannot hold being-in-itself responsible. The circumstances of his life do not compel him, since in choosing his world he chose the circumstances of his life. And insofar as he has no predetermined nature, he cannot lay responsibility for his misfortunes on innate or unconscious psychological drives. The values an individual chooses are chosen freely. Their one and only possible source is an unfettered, undictated choice of individual consciousness. Those who attribute failings, weaknesses, or misfortunes either to material or psychological determinism are profoundly mistaken. Man is totally without excuse. As the being through whom values and meanings arise, as the being through whom the world comes into existence, man is himself without justification.

It is Sartre's claim that all men have known the experience of anguish and that consequently all men have at least an implicit consciousness of their total freedom and total responsibility. It is evident, however, that most men are not explicitly conscious of the human condition as Sartre conceives it. To explain this Sartre introduces the notions of authenticity and bad faith. An authentic man is one who heeds the voice of experience and holds fast to a just conception of his nature and his relationship to the world. Most men, however, are incapable of authenticity. They do not want to believe that ultimate being is without meaning or to assume full responsibility for the circumstances of their lives. They find it more comfortable to believe that they and the world they inhabit are products of benevolent external forces. They would like to enjoy the dignity of a free being, but they cannot face up to the dreadful responsibility that goes with it. Most men, therefore, live out their lives in bad faith.

St. Anselm said even the fool knows in his heart that God exists. He regarded atheism as a kind of intellectual acrobacy—a mental trick performed by men who are too proud to admit they are created beings or too ashamed to accept their responsibility before God. Sartre turns the tables on Anselm. Theism is merely a device by which men attempt to deny their alienation from being and their freedom. At the deepest and most profound level of consciousness these men know that there is no God and that in the last analysis everything depends upon their own free choice. The proof of this is the sense of pride and shame. If a man successfully resists torture, he takes pride in his success. If he does not, he is ashamed. But if he did not have an implicit consciousness of being the incontestable and ultimate author of his behavior, how could we explain this sense of pride and shame?

Sartre's brand of existentialism differs in important respects from that of other existentialists, and in his later writing Sartre himself modified some of his earlier thinking. Many existentialists are Christians, and even the atheistic existentialists conceive of being in a variety of ways. All of them, however, stress man's freedom and responsibility. All insist upon the tragic aspects of the human condition by challenging many of the ordinary comforting illusions. And all of them value above everything else the dignity of a being who is fully conscious of his freedom and who has the courage to assume its heavy burdens. An intense and fully authentic life is not without risk; but it is better than the only possible alternative: a life of self-deception and quiet desperation.

A GUIDE

TO FURTHER

READING

THE following bibliography was devised for the beginning student. Fuller bibliographies will be found in many of the books cited below. If the name of the publisher is not listed, the book is available in several editions. Starred items are available in paperback. Double-starred items are available in Dover editions. For availability and prices visit our website at www.doverpublications.com or write to Dover Publications, Inc., 31 East 2nd Street, Mineola, New York 11501.

General Introductions

EDWARDS, PAUL, and ARTHUR PAP, eds. *A Modern Introduction to Philosophy*. Glencoe, Ill.: Free Press, 1965. A comprehensive anthology, topically arranged, with selections by classical and contemporary authors. Extensive bibliographies follow each chapter.

HOSPERS, JOHN. *An Introduction to Philosophical Analysis*. Englewood Cliffs, N.J.: Prentice-Hall, 1953. An illustration of the analytic approach by a well-known American philosopher.

PERELMAN, CH. *An Historical Introduction to Philosophical Thinking*, trans., Kenneth A. Brown. New York: Random House, 1965. A brief historical introduction by a European scholar.

RANDALL, JOHN H., JR., and JUSTUS BUCHLER. *Philosophy: An Introduction*. New York: Barnes & Noble, 1942. A brief topical introduction by two prominent pragmatists.

Classical Authors

PLATO. The most widely read of the dialogues is**The Republic; although the announced subject is justice, the dialogue also contains a statement of the theory of Ideas and an introduction to Plato's political philosophy. The **Apology, Socrates' answer to his prosecutors, and the **Phaedo, an account of Socrates' last hours, are among the most moving of the dialogues. For Plato's theory of knowledge see *Meno and **Theaetetus; for his metaphysics see *Parmenides and *Timaeus. For Plato's views on ethics see *Meno, *Protagoras, *Gorgias, and *Philebus. For his views on art see**Phaedrus; on love, the**Symposium.

ARISTOTLE. *Metaphysics,**Poetics, and**Nichomachean Ethics.

LUCRETIUS. *On the Nature of Things. This is not only the best and fullest account of Epicureanism, but also a great Roman literary classic.

AUGUSTINE.**Confessions. This is a fascinating personal account of Augustine's conversion to Christianity interspersed with philosophical reflections.

AQUINAS, THOMAS. The great works by this author are Summa Theologica and Summa Contra Gentiles. The student is advised, however, to read first a good secondary source such as Frederick C. Copleston, *Aquinas, Baltimore: Penguin Books, 1955.

DESCARTES, RENÉ. *Meditations on First Philosophy and *The Discourse on Method.

LOCKE, JOHN. The major primary source, **Essay Concerning Human Understanding, is long and difficult. Daniel J. O'Connor, *John Locke, Baltimore: Penguin Books, 1952, is a helpful introduction.

LEIBNIZ, GOTTFRIED. Theodicy, London: Routledge & Kegan Paul, 1952.

SPINOZA, BENEDICT. *Ethics and**Treatise on the Correction of the Understanding. These, too, are difficult books. Stuart Hampshire, *Spinoza, Baltimore: Penguin Books, 1952, is a good guide for the beginner.

BERKELEY, GEORGE. *Three Dialogues of Hylas and Philonous. Geoffrey J. Warnock, *Berkeley, Baltimore: Penguin Books, 1953, is an acute exposition and critique of Berkeley's system by a contemporary English analytic philosopher.

HUME, DAVID. *An Enquiry Concerning Human Understanding, *Dialogues Concerning Natural Religion, *An Enquiry Concerning the Principles of Morals, and *On Miracles.

KANT, IMMANUEL. The principal work, Critique of Pure Reason, is not recommended for beginners. *Prolegomena to Any Future Metaphysics, though itself difficult, is a more readable account of his metaphysics and theory of knowledge. For Kant's ethics, see *Fundamental Principles of the Metaphysics of Morals.

MILL, JOHN STUART. *Utilitarianism and *Nature and Utility of Religion.

Twentieth-Century Philosophy

PRAGMATISM

PEIRCE, CHARLES SANDERS. Peirce's work consists of essays, reviews, and various incomplete manuscripts published as the *Collected Papers of Charles Sanders Peirce*, eight volumes, Cambridge: Harvard University Press, 1931–58. Justus Buchler, ed., **Philosophical Writings of Peirce*, New York: Dover, 1940, is a one-volume anthology; it contains Peirce's famous essay, "How to Make Our Ideas Clear."

JAMES, WILLIAM. James published many books in his lifetime, almost all of which are eminently readable. In **Pragmatism, A New Name for Some Old Ways of Thinking*, New York: Meridian, 1955, James gives the fullest statement of his brand of pragmatism. Alburey Castell, ed., *Essays in Pragmatism*, New York: Hafner, 1948, gives a good idea of James' range of interest.**Varieties of Religious Experience* is probably James' most widely read book.

DEWEY, JOHN. *Reconstruction in Philosophy* gives Dewey's account of the historical role and proper function of philosophy. **Experience and Nature*, New York: Dover, 1958, is a difficult but indispensable work for anyone who wishes to understand his metaphysics. *The Quest for Certainty* is a good introduction to his theory of knowledge. For his ethics see**Human Nature and Conduct*.

LOGICAL POSITIVISM

Most of the basic writings of the major figures are either unavailable in English or too technical for the beginning student. A. J. Ayer,**Language, Truth, and Logic*, New York: Dover, 1946, however, is a short and lively statement of positivism that has served well as an introduction for many years.

ANALYTIC PHILOSOPHY

Bertrand Russell has written voluminously on a variety of topics both technical and popular. *Problems of Philosophy* is a semi-popular account of Russell's views in the period immediately preceding World War I. *Religion and Science* is a good example of his popular writings. The best introduction to George E. Moore is *Philosophical Papers*.

LINGUISTIC ANALYSIS

Ludwig Wittgenstein, *Philosophical Investigations*, Oxford: Blackwell, 1953, is the classic work. Gilbert Ryle, *The Concept of Mind*, Oxford: Clarendon Press, 1962, and John Austin, *Sense and Sensibilia*, are almost as well known. Perhaps, however, the best introduction is *Logic and Lan-

guage, ed., Antony Flew; this collection of essays by various authors gives a good sense of the diversity of the movement.

EXISTENTIALISM

The three great classics of existentialist literature are Kierkegaard, *Concluding Unscientific Postscript,* Princeton: Princeton University Press, 1944; Heidegger, *Being and Time,* New York: Harper & Row, 1962; and Sartre, **Being and Nothingness,* New York: Philosophical Library, 1956. All three books are long and difficult.

Among secondary sources dealing with the movement are Harold J. Blackham, **Six Existentialist Thinkers,* New York: Harper & Row, 1959, which gives brief summaries of the writings of key figures, and Robert G. Olson, ***An Introduction to Existentialism,* New York: Dover, 1962, which deals analytically with the major existentialist themes.

Though less substantial philosophically than the classic texts, the following books will go a long way toward revealing the spirit of the movement: Kierkegaard, **Fear and Trembling,* New York: Anchor, 1954; Unamuno, **The Tragic Sense of Life,* New York: Dover, 1954; and Buber, **I and Thou,* New York: Scribner's, 1937. Walter Kaufmann, **Existentialism from Dostoevsky to Sartre,* New York: Meridian, 1956, is a popular anthology.

Ethics

The great classical sources include: Plato, **Meno,* **Protagoras,* **Gorgias,* and **Philebus;* Aristotle, ***Nichomachean Ethics;* Joseph Butler, **Sermons upon Human Nature;* Hume, **An Enquiry Concerning the Principles of Morals;* Kant, **Fundamental Principles of the Metaphysics of Morals;* and Mill, **Utilitarianism.* For emotivism see Ayer, ***Language, Truth, and Logic,* Chapter VI, and Charles Stevenson, **Ethics and Language.* For contemporary analytic approaches see Paul Edwards, **The Logic of Moral Discourse* and Patrick H. Nowell-Smith, **Ethics.* For naturalistic approaches in the pragmatist tradition see John Dewey, ***Human Nature and Conduct;* Abraham Edel, *Ethical Judgment,* Glencoe, Ill.: Free Press, 1955; and Robert G. Olson, **The Morality of Self-Interest,* New York: Harcourt, Brace & World, 1965.

Religion

John Hick, ed., **The Existence of God,* New York: Macmillan, 1964, is a relatively brief anthology with an excellent annotated bibliography. William P. Alston, ed., *Religious Belief and Philosophical Thought,* New York: Harcourt, Brace & World, 1963, is more extensive.

The following books are also recommended: Augustine, **Confessions;* Frederick C. Copleston, *Aquinas;* Leibniz, *Theodicy;* Hume, *Dialogues Concerning Natural Religion* and *On Miracles;* William Paley, *Natural Theology;* Kierkegaard, *Fear and Trembling;* William James, **Varieties of Religious Experience;* C. S. Lewis, *Mere Christianity,* New York: Macmillan, 1960; and Russell, *Religion and Science.*

Metaphysics and Theory of Knowledge

For the key works of the major figures see the second and third sections of this bibliography.

For brief, nonhistorical introductions by contemporary analytic philosophers see Roderick Chisholm, *The Theory of Knowledge,* Englewood Cliffs, N.J.: Prentice-Hall, 1966; Richard Taylor, *Metaphysics,* Englewood Cliffs, N.J.: Prentice-Hall, 1965; and W. H. Walsh, *Metaphysics,* New York: Harcourt, Brace & World, 1966, a sympathetic but judicious account of traditional metaphysical schemes.

INDEX

A posteriori knowledge. *See* Empirical knowledge
A priori knowledge, 38–39. *See also* Rationalism
    Hume's analysis of, 48–49
    Kant's analysis of, 53–55
    logical positivist analysis of, 119–23
Absolute Spirit, 14–15
Actuality, as concept in Aristotle's philosophy, 67–68
Agnosticism, 7, 89
Altruism, 8. *See also* Benevolence
Analytic philosophy, 125–29
    criticism by, of emotivism, 102–03
    criticism of, by continental philosophers, 129–30
    on proper role of philosophy, 4
Analytic propositions
    Kant's analysis of, 53–54
    logical positivist analysis of, 119–23
    See also A priori knowledge
Anguish. *See* Existential anguish
Anselm, St. (1033–1109)
    on motives of atheists, 134
    ontological argument of, for existence of God, 73–76
Aquinas, St. Thomas (1225–1274)
    criticism by, of Anselm's proof for existence of God, 73, 76
    as empiricist, 44–45
    on ethics, 8, 92, 93, 100, 104
    on faith and reason, 88
    on revelation, 90

Aristotle (384–22 B.C.),   5–6, 13, 26, 113
    as empiricist,   44–45
    on ethics,   7–8, 92, 100, 104
    speculative philosophy of,   64–72
Atheism, 7
    Anselm's interpretation of,   134
    argument against existence of God,   82–86
    Sartre's interpretation of,   134
    See also God
Atomism,   14, 16–17, 18
Augustine, St. (354–430), on evil,   83
Austin, John L. (1911–60),   125
Ayer, Alfred Jules (1910–   ),   33–35
    as logical positivist,   118

Bad faith,   133–34
Beauvoir, Simone de (1911–   ),   130
Becoming, as concept in Plato's philosophy,   58
Being, as concept in Plato's philosophy,   58
Being and Nothingness,   130, 131
Being-for-itself,   131–32
Being-in-itself,   131–33
Belief,   89, 115
Benevolence
    as attribute of God,   84–85
    as motive of human behavior,   94, 108
Bentham, Jeremy (1748–1832),   92
Berdyaev, Nicholas (1874–1948),   130
Bergmann, Gustav (1906–   ),   118
Bergson, Henri (1859–1941),   111
Berkeley, George (1685–1753),   30–33, 44, 47–48, 123
Blumberg, Albert (1906–   ),   118
Bradley, Francis Herbert (1846–1924),   117
Brothers Karamasov, The,   92
Buber, Martin (1878–1965),   130
Buchler, Justus (1914–   ),   112
Buddhism,   73

Camus, Albert (1913–60),   130
Carnap, Rudolf (1891–   ),   118

Categorical imperative, 95–96
Categories of human understanding, as concept in Kant's philosophy, 56
Causality
    Aristotle's analysis of, 65–68
    Descartes' contention on, 42–43
    Hume's analysis of, 50–52
    Kant's analysis of, 55
Ceremonial utterances, 127
Change, Aristotle's analysis of, 66–67
Chestov, Léon (1868–1938), 130
Christianity, 14, 73
Clarity and distinctness, as criteria of self-evident truths, 40–42, 120
Cogito, ergo sum, 40
Coherence theory of truth, 117
Common sensibles, 26
Concepts, as opposed to images, 45–48
Connotation, as logical concept, 60
Consciousness, Sartre's interpretation of, 131–32
Correspondence theory of truth, 116–17
Cosmological argument for existence of God, 76–77
Courage, Socratic analysis of in *Laches,* 10–12
Created substances, in Descartes' philosophy, 29. *See also* Extended substance; Thinking substance
Critical philosophy, 9–13

Death, Plato's views on, 63
Defining properties, distinguished from meaning criteria, 103
Definitional statements, 120–22
Demonstrative truths, 38–39. *See also* A priori knowledge
Denotation, as logical concept, 60
Deontological ethics, 8, 91–99, 107–08
Descartes, René (1596–1650), 4, 7, 38, 53, 56, 129
    argument of, for existence of external world, 27
    argument of, for existence of God, 42, 74
    belief of, in innate ideas, 45–46
    belief of, in lower animals as automata, 130
    as Christian, 32, 74
    criticism of, by logical positivists, 120
    as dualist, 7, 29–30
    as rationalist, 5, 37–40
    as representationalist, 22–30

Descriptive meaning, as opposed to emotive meaning,   102
Determinism, and problem of human freedom and moral responsibility,
    109–10
Dewey, John (1859–1952)
    on ethics,   105–07
    as exponent of pragmatism,   112, 115–16
    on role of philosophy,   4
Dialectic. *See* Hegelian dialectic; Platonic dialectic
Dostoievsky, Feodor (1821–1881),   92–93
Dreams, epistemological problem of,   19–20, 21, 23

Efficient causes,   65, 67, 71–72
Egoism. *See* Ethical egoism
Einstein, Albert (1879–1955),   16, 122
Elements, as concept in Aristotle's philosophy,   67
Emotive meaning, as opposed to descriptive meaning,   102
Emotivism,   102–03
    criticism of, by analytic philosophers,   102, 127–28
Empirical knowledge,   38
    Hume's analysis of,   50
    logical positivist analysis of,   123–25
    pragmatist analysis of,   112–17
    See also Empiricism
Empirical terms, as logical concept,   120–22
Empiricism,   5
    classical,   44–52
    and positivism,   118–23
    and pragmatism,   111–17
    and representationalism,   28
    in response to challenge of Kant,   54–55
Entelechy, as concept in Aristotle's philosophy,   67–68
Epicurus (342?–270 B.C.)
    as atomist,   14, 18
    on ethics,   7, 18, 92
Errors of sense, epistemological problem of,   20, 21–22
Esse est percipii,   32
Esthetics,   9
Ether, as concept in Aristotle's philosophy,   67
Ethical altruism,   8
Ethical egoism,   8

Ethics, 38
Euclidean geometry
    logical positivist interpretation of, 122–23
    and Plato's theory of ideas, 59
    status of postulates of, 41
Eudaemonism, 7, 100–01
Euthyphro, 12
Evil, problem of, 82–86
Evolutionism, as influence on pragmatist thinking, 112–13
"Exist," as pseudo-predicate, 75–76
Existential anguish, 131–32
Existentialism, 129–34
    on role of philosophy, 4
Experience, as concept in empiricist epistemology, 44–48
Experimentation, importance of, in science, 17
Extended substance, 29, 31

Facticity, 131–32
Faith, 86–90
Family resemblance of words, 103
Feigl, Herbert (1902–   ), 118
Final causes, 65, 67–72
"First philosophy," 6
Formal cause, as concept in Aristotle's philosophy, 65–66
Forms. *See* Platonic Forms
Forms of sensibility, as concept in Kant's philosophy, 56
Freedom
    existentialist interpretation of, 133–34
    and moral responsibility, 107–10
    as supreme value and cause of evil, 85–86
Freud, Sigmund (1856–1939), 104

Galileo (1564–1642), 27–28
God
    arguments for existence of, 42, 73–82
    argument for nonexistence of, 82–86
    Aristotle's concept of, as Unmoved Mover, 69–70, 71–72
    as creator of physical world, 32
    as immanent or transcendent, 7

Plato's concept of,   73, 78
as premise in Descartes' proof of existence of external world,   27
Spinoza's concept of,   73
as uncreated substance in Descartes' philosophy,   28–29
Good, nature of, 99–107

Hallucinations, epistemological problem of,   19–20, 21, 23
Happiness,   99–101
Heavens, Aristotle's theory of,   66–67, 69–70
Hedonism,   7, 100–01
Hegel, Georg Wilhelm Friedrich (1770–1831),   14–15, 129
Hegelian dialectic,   15
Heidegger, Martin (1889–   ),   130
Human condition, the,   4, 131–34
Hume, David (1711–76)
    on causality,   50–52
    criticism by, of Anselm's argument for existence of God,   74–75
    criticism by, of concept of substance,   29, 33
    as empiricist,   5, 44–50, 118, 120
    on freedom and moral responsibility,   109
    on miracles,   80–81
    on nature of belief,   89
Husserl, Edmund (1859–1938),   111
Hypothetical entities in science and philosophy,   16–17
Hypothetical imperatives,   95

Idea
    as name for all mental contents,   23, 33
    as opposed to experience or sensation,   44–47
Ideas. See Platonic Forms
Images, as opposed to concepts,   44–47
Immanence of God,   7, 73
Immortality, Plato's proof of,   62–63
Inauthenticity,   133–34
Indubitability, as criterion of self-evident truths in Descartes' philosophy,
        40–41, 120
Infinite regress,   76–77
Instrumental goods,   99–100
Instrumentalism,   112. See also Pragmatism

Intellectual evil, 82
Intellectualists, 85
Intelligence
    pragmatist interpretation of, 112–13
    role of, in Dewey's ethics, 105–07
Intrinsic goods, 99–107
Intuitive knowledge, 38

James, William (1842–1910)
    as pluralist, 6, 13
    as pragmatist, 111–17
    on traditional theological concepts of God, 77
Jaspers, Karl (1883–   ), 130

Kant, Immanuel (1724–1804)
    and concept of noumenal and phenomenal worlds, 56, 132–33
    criticism by, of Anselm's argument for existence of God, 74–75
    epistemology of, 52–56, 119–20
    on ethics, 8, 92, 95–96, 108
Kepler, Johannes (1571–1630), 27–28, 38
Kierkegaard, Søren (1813–55), 87, 130
Khrushchev, Nikita (1894–   ), 97

Laches, 10–11
Learning, as reminiscence in Plato's philosophy, 62–63
Leibniz, Gottfried Wilhelm (1646–1716)
    as rationalist, 38, 56
    on religion, 74, 84–85
Lewis, Clarence Irving (1883–1964), 112
Libertarianism, 109
Linguistic philosophy. See Analytic philosophy
Locke, John (1632–1704), 129
    as empiricist, 44–46, 55
    as representationalist, 22–23, 28, 30, 32
Logic, 9
    informal, of language, 126–28
    logical positivist interpretation of, 123–25
    Mill, John Stuart, interpretation of, by, 39

Logical constructs, 34
Logical empiricism. *See* Logical positivism
Logical positivism, 117–25
    criticism of, by analytic philosophers, 125–29
    on role of philosophy, 3–4
Logical statements, as opposed to empirical statements, 120–23
Logical terms, as opposed to empirical terms, 120–22
Lucretius (96?–55 B.C.), 14, 18

Malin génie, 40
Marcel, Gabriel (1889–   ), 130
Marxism, 4, 14
Material causes, as concept in Aristotle's philosophy, 65–66
Mathematical Principles of Natural Philosophy, 3
Mathematics
    as model of genuine knowledge in rationalist epistemology, 5, 38, 39, 59
    role of, in science, 17, 27
    Kant's analysis of, 54
    logical positivist interpretation of, 123–25
Mead, Herbert (1863–1931), 112
Meaning criteria, as distinguished from defining properties, 103
Meno, 63
Merleau-Ponty, Maurice (1908–61), 130
Metaphysical good, 84
Metaphysical idealism, 7, 30–34
Metaphysics, 6, 64, 69
Mill, John Stuart (1806–73)
    on ethics, 7, 8, 92, 96, 108
    position of, on logical and mathematic truths, 39
Mind and matter, problem of, 6–7, 29–30
Miracles, 79–82
Monism, 6, 78–79, 117
Moore, George Edward (1873–1958), 101–02, 125
Moral evil, 82
Moral responsibility, 107–10
Moral rules. *See* Right and wrong

Nagel, Ernest (1901–   ), 112
Naive realism, 7, 21–22

Naturalistic fallacy, 101
Neo-Thomism, 71–72, 100, 105, 111
Neurath, Otto (1882–1945), 118
Newton, Sir Isaac (1642–1727), 3, 16, 53, 77
Nietzsche, Friedrich Wilhelm (1844–1900), 130
Noumena, 56, 131–32

Objective right. *See* Right and wrong
Occasionalism, 30
Omnipotence, as attribute of God, 85–86
Ontological argument for existence of God, 73–76
Ontology, 6
Opinion, as distinguished from knowledge, 5
Ordinary language philosophy. *See* Analytic philosophy

Parmenides, 60–61, 64
Pascal, Blaise (1623–62), 89–90
Peirce, Charles Sanders (1839–1914), 6, 111–15
Perception. *See* Experience; Sensation
Performatory utterances, 127
Phaedo, 63
Phenomena, 56, 132–33
Phenomenalism, 33–35
Phenomenology, 111
Physical evil, 82
Piety, Socrates' analysis of, in *Euthyphro,* 12–13
Plato (427?–347 B.C.), 5, 10, 38, 64, 72
    and his concept of God, 73, 78
    as influence on Aristotle, 70–71
    speculative philosophy of, 57–63
    See also Socrates
Platonic dialectic, 10
Platonic Forms, 58–62
Pleasure. *See* Hedonism
Pluralism, 6, 79, 117
Positivism. *See* Logical positivism
Positivist program, 125
Potentiality, as concept in Aristotle's philosophy, 67–68
Pragmaticism, 112

Pragmatism
    epistemology of, 111–17
    ethics of,   105–07
    pluralistic metaphysics of,   4, 6, 117
Pragmatist theory of truth,   114–17
Preexistence, Plato's theory of,   62
Primary qualities,   24–27, 31
Principia Mathematica,   123
Problem of evil,   82–86
Promises,   96
Protocol statements,   124
Pythagoreans,   38

Rationalism,   5
    Cartesian,   37–44
    and coherence theory of truth,   117
Reincarnation, Plato's theory of,   62
Reminiscence, Plato's theory of learning as,   62–63
Representationalism,   22–30
    criticism of, by Berkeley,   30–32
    criticism of, by phenomenalists,   33–34
Revelation,   90
Right and wrong,   91–99, 107–10
Ross, W. D. (1877–   ),   95
Royce, Josiah (1855–1916),   117
Rule utilitarianism,   95
Russell, Bertrand (1872–   ),   3, 123, 125
Ryle, Gilbert (1900–   ),   125

St. Anselm. *See* Anselm, St.
St. Augustine (354–430),   83
St. Thomas. *See* Aquinas, St. Thomas
Santayana, George (1863–1952),   111
Sartre, Jean-Paul (1905–   ),   130–34
    Being and Nothingness by,   130, 131
Schlick, Moritz (1882–1936),   118, 124
Science
    logical positivists as philosophers of,   3–4, 128
    and philosophy,   3–4, 13, 15–18
    and representationalism,   25–27

Scientific method, Dewey's views on,   115–16
Secondary qualities,   24–27
Self-evident truths,   38. *See also* Analytic propositions
Sensation, and relative importance of sense organs,   24–27. *See also* Experience
Sense contents,   34
Sense data,   34
Socrates (470?–399 B.C.),   5, 9–13, 58, 108. *See also* Plato
Socratic irony,   9
Socratic method,   63
Solipsism,   34
Soul
    Aristotle's theory of,   70–71
    atomist theory of,   14
    Plato's theory of,   62–63
    See also Thinking substance
Speculation, as highest good in Aristotle's philosophy,   71
Speculative philosophy,   13–15
Spinoza, Benedict (1632–1677),   6, 38, 56, 74
Stalin, Joseph (1879–1953),   97
Subjective idealism. *See* Metaphysical idealism
Subjective right. *See* Right and wrong
Substance,   28–29. *See also* Extended substance; Thinking substance
Symposium,   63
Synthetic knowledge, as defined by Kant,   53–54

Tabula rasa,   45
Teleological argument for existence of God,   77–79
Teleological ethics,   8, 90–99, 107–08
Theism. *See* God
Theological virtues,   8
Thinking substance,   29, 33, 41
Third Man argument,   61
Thisness,   66
Tractatus Logico-Philosophicus,   118
Transcendence
    of God,   7, 73
    of Platonic Ideas,   58–60
Transmigration, Plato's theory of,   62
Trinity,   87, 88

Truman, Harry S (1884–   ),   98, 108
Truth, theories of,   114–17

Unamuno, Miguel de (1864–1936),   130
Unmoved Mover,   69–70, 76–77
Utilitarianism,   92–93

Values. *See* Good, nature of
Verification principle of meaning,   123–25
    criticisms of, by analytic philosophers,   126-27
    and problem of faith,   88
Vienna Circle, the,   117–18
Voluntarists,   85

Whatness,   66
Whitehead, Alfred North (1861–1947),   111, 123
Wittgenstein, Ludwig (1889–1951),   118, 125

A CATALOG OF SELECTED
DOVER BOOKS
IN ALL FIELDS OF INTEREST

A CATALOG OF SELECTED DOVER
BOOKS IN ALL FIELDS OF INTEREST

CONCERNING THE SPIRITUAL IN ART, Wassily Kandinsky. Pioneering work by father of abstract art. Thoughts on color theory, nature of art. Analysis of earlier masters. 12 illustrations. 80pp. of text. 5⅜ x 8½. 0-486-23411-8

CELTIC ART: The Methods of Construction, George Bain. Simple geometric techniques for making Celtic interlacements, spirals, Kells-type initials, animals, humans, etc. Over 500 illustrations. 160pp. 9 x 12. (Available in U.S. only.) 0-486-22923-8

AN ATLAS OF ANATOMY FOR ARTISTS, Fritz Schider. Most thorough reference work on art anatomy in the world. Hundreds of illustrations, including selections from works by Vesalius, Leonardo, Goya, Ingres, Michelangelo, others. 593 illustrations. 192pp. 7⅛ x 10¼. 0-486-20241-0

CELTIC HAND STROKE-BY-STROKE (Irish Half-Uncial from "The Book of Kells"): An Arthur Baker Calligraphy Manual, Arthur Baker. Complete guide to creating each letter of the alphabet in distinctive Celtic manner. Covers hand position, strokes, pens, inks, paper, more. Illustrated. 48pp. 8¼ x 11. 0-486-24336-2

EASY ORIGAMI, John Montroll. Charming collection of 32 projects (hat, cup, pelican, piano, swan, many more) specially designed for the novice origami hobbyist. Clearly illustrated easy-to-follow instructions insure that even beginning papercrafters will achieve successful results. 48pp. 8¼ x 11. 0-486-27298-2

BLOOMINGDALE'S ILLUSTRATED 1886 CATALOG: Fashions, Dry Goods and Housewares, Bloomingdale Brothers. Famed merchants' extremely rare catalog depicting about 1,700 products: clothing, housewares, firearms, dry goods, jewelry, more. Invaluable for dating, identifying vintage items. Also, copyright-free graphics for artists, designers. Co-published with Henry Ford Museum & Greenfield Village. 160pp. 8¼ x 11. 0-486-25780-0

THE ART OF WORLDLY WISDOM, Baltasar Gracian. "Think with the few and speak with the many," "Friends are a second existence," and "Be able to forget" are among this 1637 volume's 300 pithy maxims. A perfect source of mental and spiritual refreshment, it can be opened at random and appreciated either in brief or at length. 128pp. 5⅜ x 8½. 0-486-44034-6

JOHNSON'S DICTIONARY: A Modern Selection, Samuel Johnson (E. L. McAdam and George Milne, eds.). This modern version reduces the original 1755 edition's 2,300 pages of definitions and literary examples to a more manageable length, retaining the verbal pleasure and historical curiosity of the original. 480pp. 5³⁄₁₆ x 8¼. 0-486-44089-3

ADVENTURES OF HUCKLEBERRY FINN, Mark Twain, Illustrated by E. W. Kemble. A work of eternal richness and complexity, a source of ongoing critical debate, and a literary landmark, Twain's 1885 masterpiece about a barefoot boy's journey of self-discovery has enthralled readers around the world. This handsome clothbound reproduction of the first edition features all 174 of the original black-and-white illustrations. 368pp. 5⅜ x 8½. 0-486-44322-1

CATALOG OF DOVER BOOKS

STICKLEY CRAFTSMAN FURNITURE CATALOGS, Gustav Stickley and L. & J. G. Stickley. Beautiful, functional furniture in two authentic catalogs from 1910. 594 illustrations, including 277 photos, show settles, rockers, armchairs, reclining chairs, bookcases, desks, tables. 183pp. 6½ x 9¼. 0-486-23838-5

AMERICAN LOCOMOTIVES IN HISTORIC PHOTOGRAPHS: 1858 to 1949, Ron Ziel (ed.). A rare collection of 126 meticulously detailed official photographs, called "builder portraits," of American locomotives that majestically chronicle the rise of steam locomotive power in America. Introduction. Detailed captions. xi+ 129pp. 9 x 12. 0-486-27393-8

AMERICA'S LIGHTHOUSES: An Illustrated History, Francis Ross Holland, Jr. Delightfully written, profusely illustrated fact-filled survey of over 200 American light-houses since 1716. History, anecdotes, technological advances, more. 240pp. 8 x 10¾. 0-486-25576-X

TOWARDS A NEW ARCHITECTURE, Le Corbusier. Pioneering manifesto by founder of "International School." Technical and aesthetic theories, views of industry, eco-nomics, relation of form to function, "mass-production split" and much more. Profusely illustrated. 320pp. 6⅛ x 9¼. (Available in U.S. only.) 0-486-25023-7

HOW THE OTHER HALF LIVES, Jacob Riis. Famous journalistic record, expos-ing poverty and degradation of New York slums around 1900, by major social reformer. 100 striking and influential photographs. 233pp. 10 x 7⅞. 0-486-22012-5

FRUIT KEY AND TWIG KEY TO TREES AND SHRUBS, William M. Harlow. One of the handiest and most widely used identification aids. Fruit key covers 120 deciduous and evergreen species; twig key 160 deciduous species. Easily used. Over 300 photographs. 126pp. 5⅜ x 8½. 0-486-20511-8

COMMON BIRD SONGS, Dr. Donald J. Borror. Songs of 60 most common U.S. birds: robins, sparrows, cardinals, bluejays, finches, more—arranged in order of increasing complexity. Up to 9 variations of songs of each species.
Cassette and manual 0-486-99911-4

ORCHIDS AS HOUSE PLANTS, Rebecca Tyson Northen. Grow cattleyas and many other kinds of orchids—in a window, in a case, or under artificial light. 63 illus-trations. 148pp. 5⅜ x 8½. 0-486-23261-1

MONSTER MAZES, Dave Phillips. Masterful mazes at four levels of difficulty. Avoid deadly perils and evil creatures to find magical treasures. Solutions for all 32 exciting illustrated puzzles. 48pp. 8¼ x 11. 0-486-26005-4

MOZART'S DON GIOVANNI (DOVER OPERA LIBRETTO SERIES), Wolfgang Amadeus Mozart. Introduced and translated by Ellen H. Bleiler. Standard Italian libretto, with complete English translation. Convenient and thoroughly portable—an ideal companion for reading along with a recording or the performance itself. Introduction. List of characters. Plot summary. 121pp. 5¼ x 8½. 0-486-24944-1

FRANK LLOYD WRIGHT'S DANA HOUSE, Donald Hoffmann. Pictorial essay of residential masterpiece with over 160 interior and exterior photos, plans, eleva-tions, sketches and studies. 128pp. 9¹/₄ x 10¾. 0-486-29120-0

THE CLARINET AND CLARINET PLAYING, David Pino. Lively, comprehensive work features suggestions about technique, musicianship, and musical interpretation, as well as guidelines for teaching, making your own reeds, and preparing for public performance. Includes an intriguing look at clarinet history. "A godsend," *The Clarinet,* Journal of the International Clarinet Society. Appendixes. 7 illus. 320pp. 5⅜ x 8½. 0-486-40270-3

HOLLYWOOD GLAMOR PORTRAITS, John Kobal (ed.). 145 photos from 1926-49. Harlow, Gable, Bogart, Bacall; 94 stars in all. Full background on photographers, technical aspects. 160pp. 8⅜ x 11¼. 0-486-23352-9

THE RAVEN AND OTHER FAVORITE POEMS, Edgar Allan Poe. Over 40 of the author's most memorable poems: "The Bells," "Ulalume," "Israfel," "To Helen," "The Conqueror Worm," "Eldorado," "Annabel Lee," many more. Alphabetic lists of titles and first lines. 64pp. 5$^{3}/_{16}$ x 8¼. 0-486-26685-0

PERSONAL MEMOIRS OF U. S. GRANT, Ulysses Simpson Grant. Intelligent, deeply moving firsthand account of Civil War campaigns, considered by many the finest military memoirs ever written. Includes letters, historic photographs, maps and more. 528pp. 6⅛ x 9¼. 0-486-28587-1

ANCIENT EGYPTIAN MATERIALS AND INDUSTRIES, A. Lucas and J. Harris. Fascinating, comprehensive, thoroughly documented text describes this ancient civilization's vast resources and the processes that incorporated them in daily life, including the use of animal products, building materials, cosmetics, perfumes and incense, fibers, glazed ware, glass and its manufacture, materials used in the mummification process, and much more. 544pp. 6⅛ x 9¼. (Available in U.S. only.) 0-486-40446-3

RUSSIAN STORIES/RUSSKIE RASSKAZY: A Dual-Language Book, edited by Gleb Struve. Twelve tales by such masters as Chekhov, Tolstoy, Dostoevsky, Pushkin, others. Excellent word-for-word English translations on facing pages, plus teaching and study aids, Russian/English vocabulary, biographical/critical introductions, more. 416pp. 5⅜ x 8½. 0-486-26244-8

PHILADELPHIA THEN AND NOW: 60 Sites Photographed in the Past and Present, Kenneth Finkel and Susan Oyama. Rare photographs of City Hall, Logan Square, Independence Hall, Betsy Ross House, other landmarks juxtaposed with contemporary views. Captures changing face of historic city. Introduction. Captions. 128pp. 8¼ x 11. 0-486-25790-8

NORTH AMERICAN INDIAN LIFE: Customs and Traditions of 23 Tribes, Elsie Clews Parsons (ed.). 27 fictionalized essays by noted anthropologists examine religion, customs, government, additional facets of life among the Winnebago, Crow, Zuni, Eskimo, other tribes. 480pp. 6⅛ x 9¼. 0-486-27377-6

TECHNICAL MANUAL AND DICTIONARY OF CLASSICAL BALLET, Gail Grant. Defines, explains, comments on steps, movements, poses and concepts. 15-page pictorial section. Basic book for student, viewer. 127pp. 5⅜ x 8½. 0-486-21843-0

THE MALE AND FEMALE FIGURE IN MOTION: 60 Classic Photographic Sequences, Eadweard Muybridge. 60 true-action photographs of men and women walking, running, climbing, bending, turning, etc., reproduced from rare 19th-century masterpiece. vi + 121pp. 9 x 12. 0-486-24745-7

ANIMALS: 1,419 Copyright-Free Illustrations of Mammals, Birds, Fish, Insects, etc., Jim Harter (ed.). Clear wood engravings present, in extremely lifelike poses, over 1,000 species of animals. One of the most extensive pictorial sourcebooks of its kind. Captions. Index. 284pp. 9 x 12. 0-486-23766-4

1001 QUESTIONS ANSWERED ABOUT THE SEASHORE, N. J. Berrill and Jacquelyn Berrill. Queries answered about dolphins, sea snails, sponges, starfish, fishes, shore birds, many others. Covers appearance, breeding, growth, feeding, much more. 305pp. 5¼ x 8¼. 0-486-23366-9

ATTRACTING BIRDS TO YOUR YARD, William J. Weber. Easy-to-follow guide offers advice on how to attract the greatest diversity of birds: birdhouses, feeders, water and waterers, much more. 96pp. 5³⁄₁₆ x 8¼. 0-486-28927-3

MEDICINAL AND OTHER USES OF NORTH AMERICAN PLANTS: A Historical Survey with Special Reference to the Eastern Indian Tribes, Charlotte Erichsen-Brown. Chronological historical citations document 500 years of usage of plants, trees, shrubs native to eastern Canada, northeastern U.S. Also complete identifying information. 343 illustrations. 544pp. 6½ x 9¼. 0-486-25951-X

STORYBOOK MAZES, Dave Phillips. 23 stories and mazes on two-page spreads: Wizard of Oz, Treasure Island, Robin Hood, etc. Solutions. 64pp. 8¼ x 11.
0-486-23628-5

AMERICAN NEGRO SONGS: 230 Folk Songs and Spirituals, Religious and Secular, John W. Work. This authoritative study traces the African influences of songs sung and played by black Americans at work, in church, and as entertainment. The author discusses the lyric significance of such songs as "Swing Low, Sweet Chariot," "John Henry," and others and offers the words and music for 230 songs. Bibliography. Index of Song Titles. 272pp. 6½ x 9¼. 0-486-40271-1

MOVIE-STAR PORTRAITS OF THE FORTIES, John Kobal (ed.). 163 glamor, studio photos of 106 stars of the 1940s: Rita Hayworth, Ava Gardner, Marlon Brando, Clark Gable, many more. 176pp. 8⅜ x 11¼. 0-486-23546-7

YEKL and THE IMPORTED BRIDEGROOM AND OTHER STORIES OF YIDDISH NEW YORK, Abraham Cahan. Film Hester Street based on *Yekl* (1896). Novel, other stories among first about Jewish immigrants on N.Y.'s East Side. 240pp. 5⅜ x 8½. 0-486-22427-9

SELECTED POEMS, Walt Whitman. Generous sampling from *Leaves of Grass.* Twenty-four poems include "I Hear America Singing," "Song of the Open Road," "I Sing the Body Electric," "When Lilacs Last in the Dooryard Bloom'd," "O Captain! My Captain!"–all reprinted from an authoritative edition. Lists of titles and first lines. 128pp. 5³⁄₁₆ x 8¼. 0-486-26878-0

SONGS OF EXPERIENCE: Facsimile Reproduction with 26 Plates in Full Color, William Blake. 26 full-color plates from a rare 1826 edition. Includes "The Tyger," "London," "Holy Thursday," and other poems. Printed text of poems. 48pp. 5¼ x 7.
0-486-24636-1

THE BEST TALES OF HOFFMANN, E. T. A. Hoffmann. 10 of Hoffmann's most important stories: "Nutcracker and the King of Mice," "The Golden Flowerpot," etc. 458pp. 5⅜ x 8½. 0-486-21793-0

THE BOOK OF TEA, Kakuzo Okakura. Minor classic of the Orient: entertaining, charming explanation, interpretation of traditional Japanese culture in terms of tea ceremony. 94pp. 5⅜ x 8½. 0-486-20070-1

FRENCH STORIES/CONTES FRANÇAIS: A Dual-Language Book, Wallace Fowlie. Ten stories by French masters, Voltaire to Camus: "Micromegas" by Voltaire; "The Atheist's Mass" by Balzac; "Minuet" by de Maupassant; "The Guest" by Camus, six more. Excellent English translations on facing pages. Also French-English vocabulary list, exercises, more. 352pp. 5⅜ x 8½. 0-486-26443-2

CHICAGO AT THE TURN OF THE CENTURY IN PHOTOGRAPHS: 122 Historic Views from the Collections of the Chicago Historical Society, Larry A. Viskochil. Rare large-format prints offer detailed views of City Hall, State Street, the Loop, Hull House, Union Station, many other landmarks, circa 1904-1913. Introduction. Captions. Maps. 144pp. 9⅜ x 12¼. 0-486-24656-6

OLD BROOKLYN IN EARLY PHOTOGRAPHS, 1865-1929, William Lee Younger. Luna Park, Gravesend race track, construction of Grand Army Plaza, moving of Hotel Brighton, etc. 157 previously unpublished photographs. 165pp. 8⅞ x 11¾. 0-486-23587-4

THE MYTHS OF THE NORTH AMERICAN INDIANS, Lewis Spence. Rich anthology of the myths and legends of the Algonquins, Iroquois, Pawnees and Sioux, prefaced by an extensive historical and ethnological commentary. 36 illustrations. 480pp. 5⅜ x 8½. 0-486-25967-6

AN ENCYCLOPEDIA OF BATTLES: Accounts of Over 1,560 Battles from 1479 B.C. to the Present, David Eggenberger. Essential details of every major battle in recorded history from the first battle of Megiddo in 1479 B.C. to Grenada in 1984. List of Battle Maps. New Appendix covering the years 1967-1984. Index. 99 illustrations. 544pp. 6½ x 9¼. 0-486-24913-1

SAILING ALONE AROUND THE WORLD, Captain Joshua Slocum. First man to sail around the world, alone, in small boat. One of great feats of seamanship told in delightful manner. 67 illustrations. 294pp. 5⅜ x 8½. 0-486-20326-3

ANARCHISM AND OTHER ESSAYS, Emma Goldman. Powerful, penetrating, prophetic essays on direct action, role of minorities, prison reform, puritan hypocrisy, violence, etc. 271pp. 5⅜ x 8½. 0-486-22484-8

MYTHS OF THE HINDUS AND BUDDHISTS, Ananda K. Coomaraswamy and Sister Nivedita. Great stories of the epics; deeds of Krishna, Shiva, taken from puranas, Vedas, folk tales; etc. 32 illustrations. 400pp. 5⅜ x 8½. 0-486-21759-0

MY BONDAGE AND MY FREEDOM, Frederick Douglass. Born a slave, Douglass became outspoken force in antislavery movement. The best of Douglass' autobiographies. Graphic description of slave life. 464pp. 5⅜ x 8½. 0-486-22457-0

FOLLOWING THE EQUATOR: A Journey Around the World, Mark Twain. Fascinating humorous account of 1897 voyage to Hawaii, Australia, India, New Zealand, etc. Ironic, bemused reports on peoples, customs, climate, flora and fauna, politics, much more. 197 illustrations. 720pp. 5⅜ x 8½. 0-486-26113-1

THE PEOPLE CALLED SHAKERS, Edward D. Andrews. Definitive study of Shakers: origins, beliefs, practices, dances, social organization, furniture and crafts, etc. 33 illustrations. 351pp. 5⅜ x 8½. 0-486-21081-2

THE MYTHS OF GREECE AND ROME, H. A. Guerber. A classic of mythology, generously illustrated, long prized for its simple, graphic, accurate retelling of the principal myths of Greece and Rome, and for its commentary on their origins and significance. With 64 illustrations by Michelangelo, Raphael, Titian, Rubens, Canova, Bernini and others. 480pp. 5⅜ x 8½. 0-486-27584-1

PSYCHOLOGY OF MUSIC, Carl E. Seashore. Classic work discusses music as a medium from psychological viewpoint. Clear treatment of physical acoustics, auditory apparatus, sound perception, development of musical skills, nature of musical feeling, host of other topics. 88 figures. 408pp. 5⅜ x 8½.   0-486-21851-1

LIFE IN ANCIENT EGYPT, Adolf Erman. Fullest, most thorough, detailed older account with much not in more recent books, domestic life, religion, magic, medicine, commerce, much more. Many illustrations reproduce tomb paintings, carvings, hieroglyphs, etc. 597pp. 5⅜ x 8½.   0-486-22632-8

SUNDIALS, Their Theory and Construction, Albert Waugh. Far and away the best, most thorough coverage of ideas, mathematics concerned, types, construction, adjusting anywhere. Simple, nontechnical treatment allows even children to build several of these dials. Over 100 illustrations. 230pp. 5⅜ x 8½.   0-486-22947-5

THEORETICAL HYDRODYNAMICS, L. M. Milne-Thomson. Classic exposition of the mathematical theory of fluid motion, applicable to both hydrodynamics and aerodynamics. Over 600 exercises. 768pp. 6⅛ x 9¼.   0-486-68970-0

OLD-TIME VIGNETTES IN FULL COLOR, Carol Belanger Grafton (ed.). Over 390 charming, often sentimental illustrations, selected from archives of Victorian graphics—pretty women posing, children playing, food, flowers, kittens and puppies, smiling cherubs, birds and butterflies, much more. All copyright-free. 48pp. 9¼ x 12¼.   0-486-27269-9

PERSPECTIVE FOR ARTISTS, Rex Vicat Cole. Depth, perspective of sky and sea, shadows, much more, not usually covered. 391 diagrams, 81 reproductions of drawings and paintings. 279pp. 5⅜ x 8½.   0-486-22487-2

DRAWING THE LIVING FIGURE, Joseph Sheppard. Innovative approach to artistic anatomy focuses on specifics of surface anatomy, rather than muscles and bones. Over 170 drawings of live models in front, back and side views, and in widely varying poses. Accompanying diagrams. 177 illustrations. Introduction. Index. 144pp. 8⅜ x11¼.   0-486-26723-7

GOTHIC AND OLD ENGLISH ALPHABETS: 100 Complete Fonts, Dan X. Solo. Add power, elegance to posters, signs, other graphics with 100 stunning copyright-free alphabets: Blackstone, Dolbey, Germania, 97 more—including many lower-case, numerals, punctuation marks. 104pp. 8⅛ x 11.   0-486-24695-7

THE BOOK OF WOOD CARVING, Charles Marshall Sayers. Finest book for beginners discusses fundamentals and offers 34 designs. "Absolutely first rate . . . well thought out and well executed."–E. J. Tangerman. 118pp. 7¾ x 10⅝.   0-486-23654-4

ILLUSTRATED CATALOG OF CIVIL WAR MILITARY GOODS: Union Army Weapons, Insignia, Uniform Accessories, and Other Equipment, Schuyler, Hartley, and Graham. Rare, profusely illustrated 1846 catalog includes Union Army uniform and dress regulations, arms and ammunition, coats, insignia, flags, swords, rifles, etc. 226 illustrations. 160pp. 9 x 12.   0-486-24939-5

WOMEN'S FASHIONS OF THE EARLY 1900s: An Unabridged Republication of "New York Fashions, 1909," National Cloak & Suit Co. Rare catalog of mail-order fashions documents women's and children's clothing styles shortly after the turn of the century. Captions offer full descriptions, prices. Invaluable resource for fashion, costume historians. Approximately 725 illustrations. 128pp. 8⅜ x 11¼.

0-486-27276-1

HOW TO DO BEADWORK, Mary White. Fundamental book on craft from simple projects to five-bead chains and woven works. 106 illustrations. 142pp. 5⅜ x 8. 0-486-20697-1

THE 1912 AND 1915 GUSTAV STICKLEY FURNITURE CATALOGS, Gustav Stickley. With over 200 detailed illustrations and descriptions, these two catalogs are essential reading and reference materials and identification guides for Stickley furniture. Captions cite materials, dimensions and prices. 112pp. 6½ x 9¼. 0-486-26676-1

EARLY AMERICAN LOCOMOTIVES, John H. White, Jr. Finest locomotive engravings from early 19th century: historical (1804–74), main-line (after 1870), special, foreign, etc. 147 plates. 142pp. 11⅜ x 8¼. 0-486-22772-3

LITTLE BOOK OF EARLY AMERICAN CRAFTS AND TRADES, Peter Stockham (ed.). 1807 children's book explains crafts and trades: baker, hatter, cooper, potter, and many others. 23 copperplate illustrations. 140pp. 4⅝ x 6. 0-486-23336-7

VICTORIAN FASHIONS AND COSTUMES FROM HARPER'S BAZAR, 1867–1898, Stella Blum (ed.). Day costumes, evening wear, sports clothes, shoes, hats, other accessories in over 1,000 detailed engravings. 320pp. 9⅜ x 12¼. 0-486-22990-4

THE LONG ISLAND RAIL ROAD IN EARLY PHOTOGRAPHS, Ron Ziel. Over 220 rare photos, informative text document origin (1844) and development of rail service on Long Island. Vintage views of early trains, locomotives, stations, passengers, crews, much more. Captions. 8⅞ x 11¾. 0-486-26301-0

VOYAGE OF THE LIBERDADE, Joshua Slocum. Great 19th-century mariner's thrilling, first-hand account of the wreck of his ship off South America, the 35-foot boat he built from the wreckage, and its remarkable voyage home. 128pp. 5⅜ x 8½. 0-486-40022-0

TEN BOOKS ON ARCHITECTURE, Vitruvius. The most important book ever written on architecture. Early Roman aesthetics, technology, classical orders, site selection, all other aspects. Morgan translation. 331pp. 5⅜ x 8½. 0-486-20645-9

THE HUMAN FIGURE IN MOTION, Eadweard Muybridge. More than 4,500 stopped-action photos, in action series, showing undraped men, women, children jumping, lying down, throwing, sitting, wrestling, carrying, etc. 390pp. 7⅞ x 10⅝. 0-486-20204-6 Clothbd.

TREES OF THE EASTERN AND CENTRAL UNITED STATES AND CANADA, William M. Harlow. Best one-volume guide to 140 trees. Full descriptions, woodlore, range, etc. Over 600 illustrations. Handy size. 288pp. 4½ x 6⅜. 0-486-20395-6

GROWING AND USING HERBS AND SPICES, Milo Miloradovich. Versatile handbook provides all the information needed for cultivation and use of all the herbs and spices available in North America. 4 illustrations. Index. Glossary. 236pp. 5⅜ x 8½. 0-486-25058-X

BIG BOOK OF MAZES AND LABYRINTHS, Walter Shepherd. 50 mazes and labyrinths in all–classical, solid, ripple, and more–in one great volume. Perfect inexpensive puzzler for clever youngsters. Full solutions. 112pp. 8⅛ x 11. 0-486-22951-3

PIANO TUNING, J. Cree Fischer. Clearest, best book for beginner, amateur. Simple repairs, raising dropped notes, tuning by easy method of flattened fifths. No previous skills needed. 4 illustrations. 201pp. 5⅜ x 8½. 0-486-23267-0

HINTS TO SINGERS, Lillian Nordica. Selecting the right teacher, developing confidence, overcoming stage fright, and many other important skills receive thoughtful discussion in this indispensible guide, written by a world-famous diva of four decades' experience. 96pp. 5⅜ x 8½. 0-486-40094-8

THE COMPLETE NONSENSE OF EDWARD LEAR, Edward Lear. All nonsense limericks, zany alphabets, Owl and Pussycat, songs, nonsense botany, etc., illustrated by Lear. Total of 320pp. 5⅜ x 8½. (Available in U.S. only.) 0-486-20167-8

VICTORIAN PARLOUR POETRY: An Annotated Anthology, Michael R. Turner. 117 gems by Longfellow, Tennyson, Browning, many lesser-known poets. "The Village Blacksmith," "Curfew Must Not Ring Tonight," "Only a Baby Small," dozens more, often difficult to find elsewhere. Index of poets, titles, first lines. xxiii + 325pp. 5⅝ x 8¼. 0-486-27044-0

DUBLINERS, James Joyce. Fifteen stories offer vivid, tightly focused observations of the lives of Dublin's poorer classes. At least one, "The Dead," is considered a masterpiece. Reprinted complete and unabridged from standard edition. 160pp. 5$\frac{3}{16}$ x 8¼. 0-486-26870-5

GREAT WEIRD TALES: 14 Stories by Lovecraft, Blackwood, Machen and Others, S. T. Joshi (ed.). 14 spellbinding tales, including "The Sin Eater," by Fiona McLeod, "The Eye Above the Mantel," by Frank Belknap Long, as well as renowned works by R. H. Barlow, Lord Dunsany, Arthur Machen, W. C. Morrow and eight other masters of the genre. 256pp. 5⅜ x 8½. (Available in U.S. only.) 0-486-40436-6

THE BOOK OF THE SACRED MAGIC OF ABRAMELIN THE MAGE, translated by S. MacGregor Mathers. Medieval manuscript of ceremonial magic. Basic document in Aleister Crowley, Golden Dawn groups. 268pp. 5⅜ x 8½. 0-486-23211-5

THE BATTLES THAT CHANGED HISTORY, Fletcher Pratt. Eminent historian profiles 16 crucial conflicts, ancient to modern, that changed the course of civilization. 352pp. 5⅜ x 8½. 0-486-41129-X

NEW RUSSIAN-ENGLISH AND ENGLISH-RUSSIAN DICTIONARY, M. A. O'Brien. This is a remarkably handy Russian dictionary, containing a surprising amount of information, including over 70,000 entries. 366pp. 4½ x 6⅛. 0-486-20208-9

NEW YORK IN THE FORTIES, Andreas Feininger. 162 brilliant photographs by the well-known photographer, formerly with *Life* magazine. Commuters, shoppers, Times Square at night, much else from city at its peak. Captions by John von Hartz. 181pp. 9¼ x 10¾. 0-486-23585-8

INDIAN SIGN LANGUAGE, William Tomkins. Over 525 signs developed by Sioux and other tribes. Written instructions and diagrams. Also 290 pictographs. 111pp. 6⅛ x 9¼. 0-486-22029-X

ANATOMY: A Complete Guide for Artists, Joseph Sheppard. A master of figure drawing shows artists how to render human anatomy convincingly. Over 460 illustrations. 224pp. 8⅜ x 11¼. 0-486-27279-6

MEDIEVAL CALLIGRAPHY: Its History and Technique, Marc Drogin. Spirited history, comprehensive instruction manual covers 13 styles (ca. 4th century through 15th). Excellent photographs; directions for duplicating medieval techniques with modern tools. 224pp. 8⅜ x 11¼. 0-486-26142-5

DRIED FLOWERS: How to Prepare Them, Sarah Whitlock and Martha Rankin. Complete instructions on how to use silica gel, meal and borax, perlite aggregate, sand and borax, glycerine and water to create attractive permanent flower arrangements. 12 illustrations. 32pp. 5⅜ x 8½. 0-486-21802-3

EASY-TO-MAKE BIRD FEEDERS FOR WOODWORKERS, Scott D. Campbell. Detailed, simple-to-use guide for designing, constructing, caring for and using feeders. Text, illustrations for 12 classic and contemporary designs. 96pp. 5⅜ x 8½. 0-486-25847-5

THE COMPLETE BOOK OF BIRDHOUSE CONSTRUCTION FOR WOOD-WORKERS, Scott D. Campbell. Detailed instructions, illustrations, tables. Also data on bird habitat and instinct patterns. Bibliography. 3 tables. 63 illustrations in 15 figures. 48pp. 5¼ x 8½. 0-486-24407-5

SCOTTISH WONDER TALES FROM MYTH AND LEGEND, Donald A. Mackenzie. 16 lively tales tell of giants rumbling down mountainsides, of a magic wand that turns stone pillars into warriors, of gods and goddesses, evil hags, powerful forces and more. 240pp. 5⅜ x 8½. 0-486-29677-6

THE HISTORY OF UNDERCLOTHES, C. Willett Cunnington and Phyllis Cunnington. Fascinating, well-documented survey covering six centuries of English undergarments, enhanced with over 100 illustrations: 12th-century laced-up bodice, footed long drawers (1795), 19th-century bustles, 19th-century corsets for men, Victorian "bust improvers," much more. 272pp. 5⅜ x 8¼. 0-486-27124-2

ARTS AND CRAFTS FURNITURE: The Complete Brooks Catalog of 1912, Brooks Manufacturing Co. Photos and detailed descriptions of more than 150 now very collectible furniture designs from the Arts and Crafts movement depict davenports, settees, buffets, desks, tables, chairs, bedsteads, dressers and more, all built of solid, quarter-sawed oak. Invaluable for students and enthusiasts of antiques, Americana and the decorative arts. 80pp. 6½ x 9¼. 0-486-27471-3

WILBUR AND ORVILLE: A Biography of the Wright Brothers, Fred Howard. Definitive, crisply written study tells the full story of the brothers' lives and work. A vividly written biography, unparalleled in scope and color, that also captures the spirit of an extraordinary era. 560pp. 6⅛ x 9¼. 0-486-40297-5

THE ARTS OF THE SAILOR: Knotting, Splicing and Ropework, Hervey Garrett Smith. Indispensable shipboard reference covers tools, basic knots and useful hitches; handsewing and canvas work, more. Over 100 illustrations. Delightful reading for sea lovers. 256pp. 5⅜ x 8½. 0-486-26440-8

FRANK LLOYD WRIGHT'S FALLINGWATER: The House and Its History, Second, Revised Edition, Donald Hoffmann. A total revision—both in text and illustrations—of the standard document on Fallingwater, the boldest, most personal architectural statement of Wright's mature years, updated with valuable new material from the recently opened Frank Lloyd Wright Archives. "Fascinating"—The New York Times. 116 illustrations. 128pp. 9¼ x 10¾. 0-486-27430-6

PHOTOGRAPHIC SKETCHBOOK OF THE CIVIL WAR, Alexander Gardner. 100 photos taken on field during the Civil War. Famous shots of Manassas Harper's Ferry, Lincoln, Richmond, slave pens, etc. 244pp. 10⅝ x 8¼. 0-486-22731-6

FIVE ACRES AND INDEPENDENCE, Maurice G. Kains. Great back-to-the-land classic explains basics of self-sufficient farming. The one book to get. 95 illustrations. 397pp. 5⅜ x 8½. 0-486-20974-1

CATALOG OF DOVER BOOKS

A MODERN HERBAL, Margaret Grieve. Much the fullest, most exact, most useful compilation of herbal material. Gigantic alphabetical encyclopedia, from aconite to zedoary, gives botanical information, medical properties, folklore, economic uses, much else. Indispensable to serious reader. 161 illustrations. 888pp. 6½ x 9¼. 2-vol. set. (Available in U.S. only.)   Vol. I: 0-486-22798-7   Vol. II: 0-486-22799-5

HIDDEN TREASURE MAZE BOOK, Dave Phillips. Solve 34 challenging mazes accompanied by heroic tales of adventure. Evil dragons, people-eating plants, blood-thirsty giants, many more dangerous adversaries lurk at every twist and turn. 34 mazes, stories, solutions. 48pp. 8¼ x 11.   0-486-24566-7

LETTERS OF W. A. MOZART, Wolfgang A. Mozart. Remarkable letters show bawdy wit, humor, imagination, musical insights, contemporary musical world; includes some letters from Leopold Mozart. 276pp. 5⅜ x 8½.   0-486-22859-2

BASIC PRINCIPLES OF CLASSICAL BALLET, Agrippina Vaganova. Great Russian theoretician, teacher explains methods for teaching classical ballet. 118 illustrations. 175pp. 5⅜ x 8½.   0-486-22036-2

THE JUMPING FROG, Mark Twain. Revenge edition. The original story of The Celebrated Jumping Frog of Calaveras County, a hapless French translation, and Twain's hilarious "retranslation" from the French. 12 illustrations. 66pp. 5⅜ x 8½.
0-486-22686-7

BEST REMEMBERED POEMS, Martin Gardner (ed.). The 126 poems in this superb collection of 19th- and 20th-century British and American verse range from Shelley's "To a Skylark" to the impassioned "Renascence" of Edna St. Vincent Millay and to Edward Lear's whimsical "The Owl and the Pussycat." 224pp. 5⅜ x 8½.
0-486-27165-X

COMPLETE SONNETS, William Shakespeare. Over 150 exquisite poems deal with love, friendship, the tyranny of time, beauty's evanescence, death and other themes in language of remarkable power, precision and beauty. Glossary of archaic terms. 80pp. 5³⁄₁₆ x 8¼.   0-486-26686-9

HISTORIC HOMES OF THE AMERICAN PRESIDENTS, Second, Revised Edition, Irvin Haas. A traveler's guide to American Presidential homes, most open to the public, depicting and describing homes occupied by every American President from George Washington to George Bush. With visiting hours, admission charges, travel routes. 175 photographs. Index. 160pp. 8¼ x 11.   0-486-26751-2

THE WIT AND HUMOR OF OSCAR WILDE, Alvin Redman (ed.). More than 1,000 ripostes, paradoxes, wisecracks: Work is the curse of the drinking classes; I can resist everything except temptation; etc. 258pp. 5⅜ x 8½.   0-486-20602-5

SHAKESPEARE LEXICON AND QUOTATION DICTIONARY, Alexander Schmidt. Full definitions, locations, shades of meaning in every word in plays and poems. More than 50,000 exact quotations. 1,485pp. 6½ x 9¼. 2-vol. set.
Vol. 1: 0-486-22726-X   Vol. 2: 0-486-22727-8

SELECTED POEMS, Emily Dickinson. Over 100 best-known, best-loved poems by one of America's foremost poets, reprinted from authoritative early editions. No comparable edition at this price. Index of first lines. 64pp. 5³⁄₁₆ x 8¼.   0-486-26466-1

THE INSIDIOUS DR. FU-MANCHU, Sax Rohmer. The first of the popular mystery series introduces a pair of English detectives to their archnemesis, the diabolical Dr. Fu-Manchu. Flavorful atmosphere, fast-paced action, and colorful characters enliven this classic of the genre. 208pp. 5³⁄₁₆ x 8¼.   0-486-29898-1

THE MALLEUS MALEFICARUM OF KRAMER AND SPRENGER, translated by Montague Summers. Full text of most important witchhunter's "bible," used by both Catholics and Protestants. 278pp. 6⅝ x 10. 0-486-22802-9

SPANISH STORIES/CUENTOS ESPAÑOLES: A Dual-Language Book, Angel Flores (ed.). Unique format offers 13 great stories in Spanish by Cervantes, Borges, others. Faithful English translations on facing pages. 352pp. 5⅜ x 8½. 0-486-25399-6

GARDEN CITY, LONG ISLAND, IN EARLY PHOTOGRAPHS, 1869–1919, Mildred H. Smith. Handsome treasury of 118 vintage pictures, accompanied by carefully researched captions, document the Garden City Hotel fire (1899), the Vanderbilt Cup Race (1908), the first airmail flight departing from the Nassau Boulevard Aerodrome (1911), and much more. 96pp. 8⅞ x 11¾. 0-486-40669-5

OLD QUEENS, N.Y., IN EARLY PHOTOGRAPHS, Vincent F. Seyfried and William Asadorian. Over 160 rare photographs of Maspeth, Jamaica, Jackson Heights, and other areas. Vintage views of DeWitt Clinton mansion, 1939 World's Fair and more. Captions. 192pp. 8⅞ x 11. 0-486-26358-4

CAPTURED BY THE INDIANS: 15 Firsthand Accounts, 1750-1870, Frederick Drimmer. Astounding true historical accounts of grisly torture, bloody conflicts, relentless pursuits, miraculous escapes and more, by people who lived to tell the tale. 384pp. 5⅜ x 8½. 0-486-24901-8

THE WORLD'S GREAT SPEECHES (Fourth Enlarged Edition), Lewis Copeland, Lawrence W. Lamm, and Stephen J. McKenna. Nearly 300 speeches provide public speakers with a wealth of updated quotes and inspiration–from Pericles' funeral oration and William Jennings Bryan's "Cross of Gold Speech" to Malcolm X's powerful words on the Black Revolution and Earl of Spenser's tribute to his sister, Diana, Princess of Wales. 944pp. 5⅜ x 8⅜. 0-486-40903-1

THE BOOK OF THE SWORD, Sir Richard F. Burton. Great Victorian scholar/adventurer's eloquent, erudite history of the "queen of weapons"–from prehistory to early Roman Empire. Evolution and development of early swords, variations (sabre, broadsword, cutlass, scimitar, etc.), much more. 336pp. 6⅛ x 9¼. 0-486-25434-8

AUTOBIOGRAPHY: The Story of My Experiments with Truth, Mohandas K. Gandhi. Boyhood, legal studies, purification, the growth of the Satyagraha (nonviolent protest) movement. Critical, inspiring work of the man responsible for the freedom of India. 480pp. 5⅜ x 8½. (Available in U.S. only.) 0-486-24593-4

CELTIC MYTHS AND LEGENDS, T. W. Rolleston. Masterful retelling of Irish and Welsh stories and tales. Cuchulain, King Arthur, Deirdre, the Grail, many more. First paperback edition. 58 full-page illustrations. 512pp. 5⅜ x 8½. 0-486-26507-2

THE PRINCIPLES OF PSYCHOLOGY, William James. Famous long course complete, unabridged. Stream of thought, time perception, memory, experimental methods; great work decades ahead of its time. 94 figures. 1,391pp. 5⅜ x 8½. 2-vol. set. Vol. I: 0-486-20381-6 Vol. II: 0-486-20382-4

THE WORLD AS WILL AND REPRESENTATION, Arthur Schopenhauer. Definitive English translation of Schopenhauer's life work, correcting more than 1,000 errors, omissions in earlier translations. Translated by E. F. J. Payne. Total of 1,269pp. 5⅜ x 8½. 2-vol. set. Vol. 1: 0-486-21761-2 Vol. 2: 0-486-21762-0

CATALOG OF DOVER BOOKS

MAGIC AND MYSTERY IN TIBET, Madame Alexandra David-Neel. Experiences among lamas, magicians, sages, sorcerers, Bonpa wizards. A true psychic discovery. 32 illustrations. 321pp. 5⅜ x 8½. (Available in U.S. only.)   0-486-22682-4

THE EGYPTIAN BOOK OF THE DEAD, E. A. Wallis Budge. Complete reproduction of Ani's papyrus, finest ever found. Full hieroglyphic text, interlinear transliteration, word-for-word translation, smooth translation. 533pp. 6½ x 9¼.
                                                                      0-486-21866-X

HISTORIC COSTUME IN PICTURES, Braun & Schneider. Over 1,450 costumed figures in clearly detailed engravings–from dawn of civilization to end of 19th century. Captions. Many folk costumes. 256pp. 8⅜ x 11¾.   0-486-23150-X

MATHEMATICS FOR THE NONMATHEMATICIAN, Morris Kline. Detailed, college-level treatment of mathematics in cultural and historical context, with numerous exercises. Recommended Reading Lists. Tables. Numerous figures. 641pp. 5⅜ x 8½.
                                                                      0-486-24823-2

PROBABILISTIC METHODS IN THE THEORY OF STRUCTURES, Isaac Elishakoff. Well-written introduction covers the elements of the theory of probability from two or more random variables, the reliability of such multivariable structures, the theory of random function, Monte Carlo methods of treating problems incapable of exact solution, and more. Examples. 502pp. 5⅜ x 8½.   0-486-40691-1

THE RIME OF THE ANCIENT MARINER, Gustave Doré, S. T. Coleridge. Doré's finest work; 34 plates capture moods, subtleties of poem. Flawless full-size reproductions printed on facing pages with authoritative text of poem. "Beautiful. Simply beautiful."–*Publisher's Weekly.* 77pp. 9¼ x 12.   0-486-22305-1

SCULPTURE: Principles and Practice, Louis Slobodkin. Step-by-step approach to clay, plaster, metals, stone; classical and modern. 253 drawings, photos. 255pp. 8⅛ x 11.
                                                                      0-486-22960-2

THE INFLUENCE OF SEA POWER UPON HISTORY, 1660–1783, A. T. Mahan. Influential classic of naval history and tactics still used as text in war colleges. First paperback edition. 4 maps. 24 battle plans. 640pp. 5⅜ x 8½.   0-486-25509-3

THE STORY OF THE TITANIC AS TOLD BY ITS SURVIVORS, Jack Winocour (ed.). What it was really like. Panic, despair, shocking inefficiency, and a little heroism. More thrilling than any fictional account. 26 illustrations. 320pp. 5⅜ x 8½.
                                                                      0-486-20610-6

ONE TWO THREE . . . INFINITY: Facts and Speculations of Science, George Gamow. Great physicist's fascinating, readable overview of contemporary science: number theory, relativity, fourth dimension, entropy, genes, atomic structure, much more. 128 illustrations. Index. 352pp. 5⅜ x 8½.   0-486-25664-2

DALÍ ON MODERN ART: The Cuckolds of Antiquated Modern Art, Salvador Dalí. Influential painter skewers modern art and its practitioners. Outrageous evaluations of Picasso, Cézanne, Turner, more. 15 renderings of paintings discussed. 44 calligraphic decorations by Dalí. 96pp. 5⅜ x 8½. (Available in U.S. only.)   0-486-29220-7

ANTIQUE PLAYING CARDS: A Pictorial History, Henry René D'Allemagne. Over 900 elaborate, decorative images from rare playing cards (14th–20th centuries): Bacchus, death, dancing dogs, hunting scenes, royal coats of arms, players cheating, much more. 96pp. 9¼ x 12¼.   0-486-29265-7

CATALOG OF DOVER BOOKS

MAKING FURNITURE MASTERPIECES: 30 Projects with Measured Drawings, Franklin H. Gottshall. Step-by-step instructions, illustrations for constructing handsome, useful pieces, among them a Sheraton desk, Chippendale chair, Spanish desk, Queen Anne table and a William and Mary dressing mirror. 224pp. 8⅛ x 11¼.
0-486-29338-6

NORTH AMERICAN INDIAN DESIGNS FOR ARTISTS AND CRAFTSPEOPLE, Eva Wilson. Over 360 authentic copyright-free designs adapted from Navajo blankets, Hopi pottery, Sioux buffalo hides, more. Geometrics, symbolic figures, plant and animal motifs, etc. 128pp. 8⅜ x 11. (Not for sale in the United Kingdom.) 0-486-25341-4

THE FOSSIL BOOK: A Record of Prehistoric Life, Patricia V. Rich et al. Profusely illustrated definitive guide covers everything from single-celled organisms and dinosaurs to birds and mammals and the interplay between climate and man. Over 1,500 illustrations. 760pp. 7½ x 10⅛. 0-486-29371-8

VICTORIAN ARCHITECTURAL DETAILS: Designs for Over 700 Stairs, Mantels, Doors, Windows, Cornices, Porches, and Other Decorative Elements, A. J. Bicknell & Company. Everything from dormer windows and piazzas to balconies and gable ornaments. Also includes elevations and floor plans for handsome, private residences and commercial structures. 80pp. 9⅜ x 12¼. 0-486-44015-X

WESTERN ISLAMIC ARCHITECTURE: A Concise Introduction, John D. Hoag. Profusely illustrated critical appraisal compares and contrasts Islamic mosques and palaces—from Spain and Egypt to other areas in the Middle East. 139 illustrations. 128pp. 6 x 9. 0-486-43760-4

CHINESE ARCHITECTURE: A Pictorial History, Liang Ssu-ch'eng. More than 240 rare photographs and drawings depict temples, pagodas, tombs, bridges, and imperial palaces comprising much of China's architectural heritage. 152 halftones, 94 diagrams. 232pp. 10¾ x 9⅞. 0-486-43999-2

THE RENAISSANCE: Studies in Art and Poetry, Walter Pater. One of the most talked-about books of the 19th century, *The Renaissance* combines scholarship and philosophy in an innovative work of cultural criticism that examines the achievements of Botticelli, Leonardo, Michelangelo, and other artists. "The holy writ of beauty."—Oscar Wilde. 160pp. 5⅜ x 8½. 0-486-44025-7

A TREATISE ON PAINTING, Leonardo da Vinci. The great Renaissance artist's practical advice on drawing and painting techniques covers anatomy, perspective, composition, light and shadow, and color. A classic of art instruction, it features 48 drawings by Nicholas Poussin and Leon Battista Alberti. 192pp. 5⅜ x 8½.
0-486-44155-5

THE MIND OF LEONARDO DA VINCI, Edward McCurdy. More than just a biography, this classic study by a distinguished historian draws upon Leonardo's extensive writings to offer numerous demonstrations of the Renaissance master's achievements, not only in sculpture and painting, but also in music, engineering, and even experimental aviation. 384pp. 5⅜ x 8½. 0-486-44142-3

WASHINGTON IRVING'S RIP VAN WINKLE, Illustrated by Arthur Rackham. Lovely prints that established artist as a leading illustrator of the time and forever etched into the popular imagination a classic of Catskill lore. 51 full-color plates. 80pp. 8⅜ x 11. 0-486-44242-X

HENSCHE ON PAINTING, John W. Robichaux. Basic painting philosophy and methodology of a great teacher, as expounded in his famous classes and workshops on Cape Cod. 7 illustrations in color on covers. 80pp. 5⅜ x 8½. 0-486-43728-0

CATALOG OF DOVER BOOKS

LIGHT AND SHADE: A Classic Approach to Three-Dimensional Drawing, Mrs. Mary P. Merrifield. Handy reference clearly demonstrates principles of light and shade by revealing effects of common daylight, sunshine, and candle or artificial light on geometrical solids. 13 plates. 64pp. 5⅜ x 8½. 0-486-44143-1

ASTROLOGY AND ASTRONOMY: A Pictorial Archive of Signs and Symbols, Ernst and Johanna Lehner. Treasure trove of stories, lore, and myth, accompanied by more than 300 rare illustrations of planets, the Milky Way, signs of the zodiac, comets, meteors, and other astronomical phenomena. 192pp. 8⅜ x 11. 0-486-43981-X

JEWELRY MAKING: Techniques for Metal, Tim McCreight. Easy-to-follow instructions and carefully executed illustrations describe tools and techniques, use of gems and enamels, wire inlay, casting, and other topics. 72 line illustrations and diagrams. 176pp. 8¼ x 10⅞. 0-486-44043-5

MAKING BIRDHOUSES: Easy and Advanced Projects, Gladstone Califf. Easy-to-follow instructions include diagrams for everything from a one-room house for bluebirds to a forty-two-room structure for purple martins. 56 plates; 4 figures. 80pp. 8¾ x 6⅜. 0-486-44183-0

LITTLE BOOK OF LOG CABINS: How to Build and Furnish Them, William S. Wicks. Handy how-to manual, with instructions and illustrations for building cabins in the Adirondack style, fireplaces, stairways, furniture, beamed ceilings, and more. 102 line drawings. 96pp. 8¾ x 6⅜. 0-486-44259-4

THE SEASONS OF AMERICA PAST, Eric Sloane. From "sugaring time" and strawberry picking to Indian summer and fall harvest, a whole year's activities described in charming prose and enhanced with 79 of the author's own illustrations. 160pp. 8¼ x 11. 0-486-44220-9

THE METROPOLIS OF TOMORROW, Hugh Ferriss. Generous, prophetic vision of the metropolis of the future, as perceived in 1929. Powerful illustrations of towering structures, wide avenues, and rooftop parks–all features in many of today's modern cities. 59 illustrations. 144pp. 8¼ x 11. 0-486-43727-2

THE PATH TO ROME, Hilaire Belloc. This 1902 memoir abounds in lively vignettes from a vanished time, recounting a pilgrimage on foot across the Alps and Apennines in order to "see all Europe which the Christian Faith has saved." 77 of the author's original line drawings complement his sparkling prose. 272pp. 5⅜ x 8½. 0-486-44001-X

THE HISTORY OF RASSELAS: Prince of Abissinia, Samuel Johnson. Distinguished English writer attacks eighteenth-century optimism and man's unrealistic estimates of what life has to offer. 112pp. 5⅜ x 8½. 0-486-44094-X

A VOYAGE TO ARCTURUS, David Lindsay. A brilliant flight of pure fancy, where wild creatures crowd the fantastic landscape and demented torturers dominate victims with their bizarre mental powers. 272pp. 5⅜ x 8½. 0-486-44198-9

Paperbound unless otherwise indicated. Available at your book dealer, online at **www.doverpublications.com**, or by writing to Dept. GI, Dover Publications, Inc., 31 East 2nd Street, Mineola, NY 11501. For current price information or for free catalogs (please indicate field of interest), write to Dover Publications or log on to **www.doverpublications.com** and see every Dover book in print. Dover publishes more than 500 books each year on science, elementary and advanced mathematics, biology, music, art, literary history, social sciences, and other areas.